real

real

BECOMING A 24/7 FOLLOWER OF JESUS

JAMIE SNYDER

BETHANY HOUSE PUBLISHERS

a division of Baker Publishing Group
Minneapolis, Minnesota

Published by Bethany House Publishers
11400 Hampshire Avenue South
Bloomington, Minnesota 55438
www.bethanyhouse.com

Bethany House Publishers is a division of
Baker Publishing Group, Grand Rapids, Michigan

Printed in the United States of America

Library of Congress Cataloging-in-Publication Data
Snyder, Jamie.
    Real : becoming a 24-7 follower of Jesus / Jamie Snyder
        pages cm
    Summary: "The author shares Bible teaching and personal stories to help
readers become deeply committed followers of Jesus who are known for
their generosity, courage, joy, faith, hope, grace, and love"— Provided by the
publisher.
    ISBN 978-0-7642-1099-0 (pbk. : alk. paper)
    1. Christian life. I. Title.
BV4501.3 .S65745 2013
248.4—dc23   2013023289

Cover design by Lookout Design, Inc.

13   14   15   16   17   18   19   7   6   5   4   3   2   1

For Alex, my bride,
Cy and Cruz, my guys,
and Jesus, our King.

contents

Part Three:
The REAL Answer

foreword

A friend of mine is a missionary in South Asia, where, despite persecution, the church is growing. He was recently telling me that many of the new churches are asking tough questions of would-be followers of Jesus to make sure they are counting the cost of becoming a Christian. Here are some of the questions:

- Are you willing to leave your home?
- Are you willing to lose your job?
- Are you willing to forgive those who persecute you?
- Are you willing to be beaten and imprisoned for your faith?
- Are you willing to die for Jesus?

Were you asked questions like this before you decided to follow Jesus? I wasn't either. Maybe you were asked:

- Are you willing to raise your hand in public?
- Are you willing to repeat a prayer out loud?
- Are you willing to change your Facebook status to Christ-follower?

There is nothing wrong with these questions, but isn't there something within you, like there is within me, that wants to be challenged more deeply? I'm thankful for religious freedom and for the privilege of worshiping God without fear of persecution, but I think we all need to be willing to answer some harder questions.

This book asks some challenging questions that will help you to be honest with yourself about whether you just believe in Jesus or are truly following after him.

When reading a book about following Jesus, there is one really important question you should ask: Does the author follow Jesus?

You would think that would be a safe assumption. After all, if a person is going to write a cookbook, you'd like to think the author is a pretty decent cook. If a person is going to write a book on diet and exercise, you'd like to think the author is in good shape. But most of us have learned to be cynical enough to have some doubts. Just because someone has the right information doesn't make that person an expert.

This is what I love about the book *Real*. Jamie Snyder explains what a Christ-follower looks like and then challenges believers to live that out. But he doesn't just download information and tell you how to apply it, he tells stories of following Jesus that will inspire you to take risks and step outside your comfort zone.

So here is my question to you: Are you willing to read this book and have the courage to be honest with yourself about what it really means to follow Jesus?

Kyle Idleman

Part One

The **real** Question

1

Mona Lisa

Mona Lisa gives me the creeps. I know how strange that must sound, so let me explain.

Several years ago I used a large poster of *Mona Lisa* for a creative element in a teaching. I had bought an extra one in case something didn't go quite right. The extra *Mona Lisa* sat propped against the wall in my office for weeks. I didn't think much of her presence at first. In fact, the company was sort of nice, and she was always so quiet. However, I noticed very quickly that she wouldn't stop staring at me. When I sat at my desk, her eyes burned a hole through me. When I sat on my office couch, her eyes followed me. Every time I finished praying and looked up, she was already staring at me again. I can only hope she had closed her eyes during the prayer. *Mona Lisa* never stopped staring and never blinked once until I disposed of her.

Truth is a lot like *Mona Lisa*, or perhaps I should say, *Mona Lisa* is a lot like truth. Truth never looks away. You can pretend truth doesn't exist, you can close the eyes of your heart, you can simply turn and look the other way, but truth never looks away or blinks.

Before I go any further, let me introduce myself. My name is Jamie; I suppose you knew that much. I am a husband, a father, a pastor, a writer, and a recovering Sunday Christian.

My Sunday-focused faith began for me as a young child. I was raised in an uber-conservative Christian church in Middle America; there are hundreds just like it. Very possibly you grew up in the same church but in a different town, in a different state. I am so thankful for the foundation of God's Word I was taught as a child. But the truth is, I was also taught, through osmosis, a Sunday-centric faith. It was not just a Sunday-morning faith, but Sunday night as well. We were the hard-core Sunday-nighters. If you missed Communion on Sunday morning, you could sit in the front pew during the third verse of a certain hymn and be served Communion on Sunday night. On those hundreds of Sunday mornings and Sunday nights, the prayers were prayed, the songs were sung, and the Bible was faithfully taught. So far, so good, right? Here was the problem. I fully understood Christianity inside the church walls on Sundays, but I was never taught how the faith translated to Monday and the rest of the week, beyond following certain rules and praying before meals.

There isn't much value in placing blame; I don't think the people who served as my spiritual leaders knew any better. They were passing on the Sunday-centric faith that they had been trained to live as well. They were good at it, and so was I.

The faith I lived for almost twenty years included Jesus but was built on Sunday religious activities. Over the last decade, I have developed a faith that is built on a relationship with Jesus, but even now I occasionally wrestle with the question, "If Sunday didn't exist, would anyone know I was a follower of Jesus?"

For many years, I would have been quick to adamantly answer yes to that question. Unfortunately, the real answer was likely no. People certainly knew I was a Sunday church attendee because I was quick to advertise that behavior, but very few would have recognized me as a follower of Jesus simply by the way I lived. Hopefully now many more would be able to identify me as a follower of Jesus because of the way I live and love, but some undoubtedly still wouldn't be able to do so.

I have never been inside a confession booth, but let me use these next few lines to share some honest confession. Even as a pastor, perhaps especially because I am a pastor, Sunday can easily begin to dominate my faith. In fact, in many ways my life is measured by Sundays. At some level I spend Monday through Saturday preparing for Sunday. There are sermons to be written, services to plan, graphics to approve, volunteers to train, and videos to be produced, and all of it has to be done before Sunday. So if I am not careful, my faith can begin revolving on the axis of Sunday. As a pastor I am a bit haunted by my own question. The question I posed applies to me, but not only to me.

So what about you? If Sunday didn't exist, would anyone know you were a follower of Jesus?

The reason I pose that question is because most people conclude someone is a Christian or not based on that person's Sunday religious activities and behaviors. You may not even be inclined to advertise your faith, but inevitably if you attend church often enough, it will come out in conversation. So if Sunday didn't exist, you would no longer have a building to point to as being the place you attend church, and if you are a pastor you would no longer have a church building to point to as the place you work. If Sunday didn't exist, we would no longer be able to use our Sunday activities as evidence that we are followers of Jesus. So back to my question . . .

I don't ask it to create a feeling of guilt. Unfortunately, that tends to be our first instinct when faced with difficult questions about our faith. Though guilt is an honest reality of our lives, I have found using guilt as a motivation for change is ineffective. There are other books you can read, and when you put them down you feel beat up, or beat down, and wonder whether you will spend eternity in heaven or not. This is not intended to be one of those books.

The purpose of asking the Sunday question is twofold. First, there is always great value in honest self-reflection. We certainly should avoid self-absorption, but there is danger in failing to honestly evaluate our lives, especially in regard to our faith. When we fail to consistently evaluate our life and faith, we can all too easily drift to a place we would never intentionally go.

If you have swum in the ocean, you know you can drift without even realizing it. Often the same drift takes place in our faith. We tend to assume that because we once chose to live in tune with God's desires for our life by following Jesus, we will always and automatically continue to do so. However, nothing could be further from the truth. Just ask the man who faithfully attended church for decades and yet suddenly found himself in the midst of an extramarital affair, destroying his family, his reputation, and his faith. Ask the Christian woman who found herself trapped in a life of addiction to prescription drugs in an attempt to quench the loneliness and purposelessness of her life. Ask the longtime church leader who became wrapped in a cocoon of self-righteousness and legalism. None of these individuals or others like them intends to end up in the midst of such undesirable, dishonorable circumstances that destroy lives and families and churches, but in the absence of honest self-evaluation we are inclined to slowly drift away from a life-giving relationship with Jesus.

Second, but more important, the purpose of asking and honestly answering the Sunday question is the hope that by doing so the Holy Spirit will stir your heart and mind concerning the life Jesus invites you to live. Jesus said, "I came so that everyone would have life, and have it in its fullest" (John 10:10 CEV). Too many of us have settled for something so much less than Jesus intended. Too many who profess to be Christians have settled for a mechanical life of religion instead of a meaningful relationship with Jesus. Religion is defined by rules and regulations, but a relationship is built upon intimacy. Religion can be scheduled; relationship is spontaneous. Religion is about measuring up; relationship is about growing deeper. Religion is man-made; relationship with Jesus is God-ordained. Religion is predictable; relationship is passionate. Religion earns the applause of men; a relationship with Jesus results in the applause of heaven.

Perhaps you wonder what the Sunday question and religion have to do with each other: Simple. Religion can be reduced to one day; a relationship with Jesus cannot. Someone once said, "Religion is a cheap imitation for a relationship with Jesus."

As I write I am on vacation in Florida with my family. The first day of the trip, when we were walking to the beach, my youngest son became fascinated with a puddle of rainwater that had gathered on the walkway. He stopped and began stomping and splashing and laughing. After a few moments I began to tug his hand to start moving again because the beach and the ocean were awaiting us. He resisted and began to cry. He wanted to stay and play in the murky rain puddle when the turquoise expanse of the ocean waited.

What if that is a picture of your faith? What if you have settled for splashing around in religion instead of getting lost in the ocean of a relationship with Jesus? Yes, this question is a bit metaphorical in nature, so let me ask it another way.

If Sunday didn't exist, would anyone know *you* were a follower of Jesus?

I have wrestled with this question for a long time, and so I feel like I need to give you this fair warning: Honestly answering this question may expose an uncomfortable truth.

You can make *Mona Lisa* go away, but the truth isn't going anywhere.

⌐ Reflection/Discussion ⌐

1. Take a few minutes to evaluate your spiritual journey. Has it been defined by religion or relationship? Discuss as openly as possible.

2. Whether you notice a pattern of religion or relationship, how did the pattern begin? Was the pattern inherited, or was it developed on your own?

3. As you honestly evaluate your faith, it is important to recognize the positive aspects you would like to maintain, as well as determine aspects that need to be removed/revived/refreshed. Prayerfully consider all aspects of your faith so you will be able to make these determinations.

⌐ Prayer ⌐

Father, prepare me for this journey of self-reflection and discovery. Likely there is so much more you desire for me to know and experience, so give me eyes to see and ears to hear. I invite you to unleash a new work in my heart, mind, and soul. Have your way with me, in me, and through me. In Jesus' name.

2

Sunday Best

I'm not sure what your childhood was like, but mine was defined by rules. In our home there was a list—a long list—of Do-Nots. Some were spoken, others unspoken. Some were rational, others incredibly irrational. Either way, they were the rules.

DO NOT get up to go to the bathroom after you have gone to bed. I should've taken care of that before I went to bed, or so I was told. What if I didn't have to go before I went to bed? I should have gone anyway, or so I was told.

DO NOT get the mail out of the mailbox. Yeah, I don't understand it either.

DO NOT use any curse word or any word that could be construed as a curse word. According to that rule, here are some words that were prohibited (sorry, Mom): Darn, Dang, Gosh. Gee. Shucks. Doggonit. Dagnabit. (Sorry, I should have warned you this book was going to be R-rated.)

DO NOT wear shorts outside of the house until May or until the temperature reaches 80 degrees. Seriously. My sister and I spent hours calling the local time-and-temperature hotline only to be disappointed when the digital voice reported just 79 degrees.

DO NOT wear church clothes out to play. This was the golden rule.

I remember one Sunday when I did, in fact, wear my church shoes out to play. I knew better. I had been told time and time again not to play in my church clothes, because the last thing you would want to do is get your church clothes dirty or church shoes scuffed up (that is another book for another day)! Well, one day apparently the thought of a few moments of joy seemed to outweigh the inevitable wrath, so I went out to play in my church clothes. Cue the gloom-and-doom music now. There I was in all my glory—bright white shirt, blue slacks, and black penny loafers—playing, when I heard my mother hollering from the porch, "Jaaaaaaaaaaammmmmmmiiiiieeeee." *Why me? Why now?* I thought as I looked down at my slightly wrinkled pants and slightly scuffed shoes. At that moment I would rather have been wearing anything else in the world, even my birthday suit, but there I stood in my Sunday best. I cannot remember how the rest of the story played out, but by golly (pardon the strong language), I am sure it wasn't pretty.

Sunday best. Traditions seem to be slowly transitioning now, but for generations the standard for Sunday morning going-to-church attire was Sunday best. For some, that meant a three-piece suit. For others, a nice, clean set of overalls. It didn't really matter as long as it was your best. Now hear me, though I prefer casual dress, there is nothing wrong with wearing Sunday-best attire. However, I would contend that *Sunday best* is a phrase that applies to much more than the clothes we don on Sunday mornings. If you think about it, the way contemporary Christianity has developed, Sunday is all about our best. When you go to church, there is the expectation that you wear your *best* clothes, be on your *best* behavior, and plaster on your *best* smile no matter how you may really feel.

I think I understand why "the best"—be it clothes, behavior, or smiles—has long been the expectation for Sunday morning.

I know this is not an overwhelmingly popular statement to make, but for generations Christianity has been and is largely defined by the Sunday morning worship experience. For some, it is about choirs and orchestras. For others, it is about guitars and drum sets. For still others, no instruments are used or allowed. For some, it is about pews, robes, and stained-glass windows. For others, it is about projectors, flashy lights, and hi-def screens. For some, it is about torn jeans, T-shirts, and flip-flops. For others, it is about collared shirts, ties, and loafers. No matter how it looks or sounds or feels, for many, if not most, Christianity equates with the Sunday morning worship experience. That means, whether consciously or subconsciously, our faith usually spins on the axis of Sunday morning.

By the way, this is one reason why there is so much tension within the local church, regardless of denominational affiliation. If your entire faith revolves around a one- or two-hour worship experience on one day of the week, and every detail of it doesn't match up exactly with your needs and wants, it is all too easy to become critical. I wish I were merely writing in theory, but unfortunately, I am conveying a daily reality of the local church.

I have been privileged to serve in church leadership for nearly a decade now. In my time I have experienced and observed, up close and from a distance, many beautiful moments of compassion, grace, and humility. But less often (thankfully), I have also seen ugly moments. In my current role as lead minister of Lakeside Christian Church, I am following in the footsteps of the previous minister, who led Lakeside with a high level of integrity and character for four decades. Such a leadership transition comes with growth pains even in the best of scenarios. I mean, any time you transition from a forty-year minister to a minister who is not even close to forty years old, there are going to be some rough spots.

Early on, criticism came.

Uninvited.

Unsolicited.

Unfortunate.

But not unexpected.

The music is too loud. The lights are too dim. The bulletin is too trendy. We have to stand too long. The minister is too young. If you have been around the church long, these comments might sound familiar. (If you are new to the church, ignore the last few lines; I don't want to give you any ideas.) Now, there is always a place and time within the church to give input and constructive criticism. And in my experience, most have shared their input in healthy ways.

When people do express animosity, it can stem from unmet needs and desires, but often there is a deeper, more serious root. At some level, Sunday is the axis on which their faith spins. And when that is the root issue, there is always going to be spoiled fruit.

It would be unfair to suggest that only those who grow discontent, frustrated, and angry with the worship experience are the ones who have allowed Sunday to serve as the axis of their faith, because that is far from the truth.

In fact, I would suggest it may be more common to become Sunday-centric when the worship experience is everything you desire it to be—when the lights are just right, the volume is dialed in perfectly, and you find the stage design captivating, the preaching compelling, and the coffee tasty. When all your wants and needs are met, Sunday can easily move from being *a* worship experience during your week to being *the* worship experience of your week.

Bottom line: Whether you dread the Sunday morning experience or crave it, your faith can quietly get built on the soil called Sunday. Sunday can become the axis on which your faith spins.

Has it happened to you?

⌐ Reflection/Discussion ⌐

1. Does your faith spin on the axis of Sunday?

2. Question #1 is hard to answer objectively. By answering these next questions you may get a better indication of the answer to #1.

   • Do you find yourself more in tune with, or interested in, Jesus on Sunday than any other day of the week?

   • When you hear the word *worship*, do you immediately think of a portion of time on Sunday that involves music?

   • Do you study/read/memorize Scripture at any other time besides Sunday?

   (These questions are not intended to induce guilt, but to help you make an honest evaluation. I am wrestling with these same questions as I write them down.)

3. In the place where you worship corporately, do you feel any Sunday-best pressure? If so, how? If not, what makes you feel at ease?

⌐ Prayer ⌐

Father, I desire to live a life of faith that is built upon you and revolves around you. Help me to honestly identify whether or not my faith is in any way built on a day, or an experience, or a place. Constantly remind me that church is not a place but a people, and that worship is not only a planned experience involving music but also a lifestyle. As Romans 12 teaches, I want my entire life to be a spiritual act of worship to you. You are worthy of all praise, honor, and glory because there is no God like you. In Jesus' name.

3

Keeping Score

As humans we love to keep score. Even when the score isn't supposed to matter, it still does.

Last year I coached a basketball team of kindergarteners. Coaching that age group seemed like a good opportunity for me, since my skill level is approximately the same as that of the average kindergartener. I am not sure how much coaching actually took place, but that was my title nonetheless. The league I coached in was Christ-centered, so there was little attention given to the scoreboard, at least there wasn't supposed to be. During the game, during time-outs, during the half-time speech, the kids almost always had at least one eye on the scoreboard. The kids weren't the only ones glancing at the scoreboard. Even the coaches would incessantly check the scoreboard (the other coaches, of course).

There is something very captivating about a scoreboard, not just in kindergarten basketball but also in a life of faith. Scoreboards measure, and we humans love measurements. We measure our waists, hips, and chests. We measure our height and weight. We measure the square footage of our homes and the acreage of our lands. We measure the size of the engines in our cars and the wheels on which they ride and the miles we get per gallon of gas. We measure the size of our TV screens in terms of inches and our beds in terms of royal figures. We *love* measurements. Measurements help us to keep score, to determine success, and to attribute worth.

In terms of our faith, Sundays are measurable. You can measure how many Sundays you attend church each year or each month. You can just as easily measure how many times or how few times the other people you know attend church. You can measure how much money you put in the offering plate, how many Bible studies you have attended, how many potlucks you have participated in, and how many baptisms you have performed. But if we are not careful, Sunday measurements can start to serve as validations of our faith.

We will never need to do so, but if each one of us were required to fill out a spiritual résumé, what would you include?

- Twenty-five years of perfect church attendance
- Ten years serving as Sunday school superintendent
- Weekly or monthly Communion server
- Monthly greeter

Perhaps your résumé would look eerily similar to this one, perhaps it wouldn't. In either case, many of us would fill up the résumé with Sunday activities. So that leads us back to the original question of this book: What if Sunday didn't exist? Would the spiritual résumé be left blank? Would you gravitate toward Wednesday evening church activities to fill it up?

Again, a spiritual résumé will never be required, at least by Jesus, but the imagery is helpful in terms of identifying how we view the Sunday morning worship experience. For some of us, it may expose how we have overemphasized one day, sometimes at the expense of the others. If we are completely honest, some of us use Sunday as a scorecard.

Using Sunday as a scorecard can come in a lot of different forms. For a layperson, Sunday can be used to measure involvement, but as a minister it is easy to use Sunday as a scorecard for success. Any minister who has a pulse loves numbers. We are quick to say, "It's is not about attendance numbers," but in our weakest moments, what we mean by that is, "It's all about the numbers." I am off on Mondays, but there is not a Monday that goes by that my mind does not gravitate toward wondering about the numbers from the day before. I know that in no way does the Sunday morning attendance serve as an indication of my worth or my ability, and yet there is something inside of me that is drawn toward the numbers. As pastors, whether we like to admit it or not, we allow the attendance and offering numbers to serve as a scorecard. With those numbers we are tempted to compare our ministries with the ones on the other side of the town, or the state, or the country. Honestly, being consumed with the numbers in terms of keeping score is not something I have a great struggle with, but the temptation is always looming.

At some level numbers do matter to God. They must; a book of the Bible is called Numbers. As you study through Acts, it quotes numbers of people in the church, so someone was counting. Numbers absolutely matter to God simply because numbers represent faces, names, and stories. Unfortunately, in the church culture now, we tend to gravitate to numbers for superficial reasons.

For years it was commonplace for a scoreboard to be hung in the church building. By scoreboard I don't mean an electronic scoreboard, but a wooden board hung on the wall that had slots for numbers to be inserted. On the board you would be able to find the Sunday morning attendance, Sunday evening attendance, offering amount—and the really snazzy scoreboards even had a slot for Wednesday night attendance. I know in most cases those numbers were displayed with the best of intentions, but at some level, doing so was an indication of our desire within the church to keep score, and Sunday is the favorite metric used.

When the church first began, Sunday was the day for corporate worship. Somehow throughout the centuries, a day that was solely intended as an opportunity for worship has in the worst of cases become an opportunity to keep score.

⌐ Reflection/Discussion ⌐

1. Have there been times in your faith journey when Sunday has been reduced to being a scoreboard event? Explain.

2. Have you ever felt like other people were keeping score on themselves, and you, with regard to Sunday attendance? Give some examples.

3. There is a fine line between valuing numbers, because they represent people, and obsessing about numbers as a way of keeping score. Talk about some ways to keep the right perspective on numbers, individually and as a church.

⌐ Prayer ⌐

Father, as a church, forgive us for the times we have allowed Sunday to become reduced to a system of keeping score. Likely we have not done so consciously, but subconsciously we have to some degree. Teach us how to value numbers without allowing them to become our way of keeping score, of ourselves or others. In Jesus' name.

4

Déjà Vu

Up to this point you may think I am undermining the significance of what takes place during a corporate gathering on Sunday morning—or Saturday night, if that is your "Sunday morning." If that is what you have heard me saying, now hear me say, *That is not what I have been saying.* (Dr. Seuss inspired that line.) I am convinced the Bible clearly communicates that what takes place when we worship in a corporate setting—no matter its look or feel—cannot be duplicated, imitated, or replaced.

So how has Sunday, a day that has been held sacred by the church, in some instances become a crutch or something worse?

As the saying goes, If you don't learn from history, you're bound to repeat it. Perhaps we didn't learn our lesson—or maybe we forgot it. Whatever the reason, it seems like history has repeated itself.

In Exodus 19 we find Moses in the midst of a close encounter with God. Can you imagine? A close encounter. With God.

On the morning of the third day there was thunder and lightning, with a thick cloud over the mountain, and a very

29

loud trumpet blast. Everyone in the camp trembled. Then Moses led the people out of the camp to meet with God, and they stood at the foot of the mountain. Mount Sinai was covered with smoke, because the LORD descended on it in fire. The smoke billowed up from it like smoke from a furnace, and the whole mountain trembled violently. As the sound of the trumpet grew louder and louder, Moses spoke and the voice of God answered him.

The LORD descended to the top of Mount Sinai and called Moses to the top of the mountain. So Moses went up.

Exodus 19:16–20

Have you ever been called into the boss's office?

The principal's office?

The coach's office?

Moses was called into God's office. The top of Mount Sinai. And it was there and then that God handed down to Moses what we now affectionately (or not-so-affectionately) call the Ten Commandments.

The commandments are not complex. You couldn't possibly write *The Ten Commandments for Dummies* because they were given in the most simplistic form. Maybe God knew more about us than we give him credit for. Or maybe we just give ourselves too much credit. None of the commandments are difficult to understand, and yet one has been historically misunderstood— the fourth commandment:

Remember the Sabbath day by keeping it holy. Six days you shall labor and do all your work, but the seventh day is a Sabbath to the LORD your God. On it you shall not do any work, neither you, nor your son or daughter, nor your manservant or maidservant, nor your animals, nor the alien within your gates. For in six days the LORD made the heavens and the earth, the sea, and all that is in them, but he rested on the seventh day. Therefore the LORD blessed the Sabbath day and made it holy.

Exodus 20:8–11 NIV1984

The message was simple. Do not work. Rest. All of you. Even E.T.

So we call the Sabbath a command, but let's call it what it is: a gift.

A day off.

A chance to put up your feet and relax.

To sip on lemonade.

To take a nap.

To sleep in.

To play on the floor with the kids.

So God gave his chosen people, the Jews, one of the finest gifts one could ever imagine, the Sabbath. We typically do not associate the word *gift* with Sabbath, and yet it fits exactly. Sabbath was intended to be a God-given opportunity to rest—to be restored, to rekindle the passion for life—for one another and for God. But what was meant to be a gift quickly became something altogether different.

Over hundreds of years, Jewish leaders developed their own system of laws based upon the laws that God had handed down. The laws, numbering in the hundreds, were written with the best of intentions: to put barriers in place not only to keep people from breaking God's law but to make sure no one ever even came close to breaking God's law. So they essentially made laws about laws about laws. Sound familiar?

The Sabbath was the central focus of many of the rules and regulations that were devised by the religious leaders. *Rest* was not a definitive enough term for them; it left too much to question. So they put in hours of hard work to define rest. Ironic.

The result of all that hard work? A seemingly endless list of rules to ensure that people really were resting as they had been commanded to do. Again, ironic.

There is not enough room in a book like this, or any book for that matter, to include an exhaustive list of all the Sabbath rules, especially an interpretation of those rules. The rules were organized into thirty-nine general categories of prohibitions called the Melakhot, but then each category could be broken down and applied in hundreds of ways. Like most laws, it may have been written in black and white, but it was anything but. It was shades of gray. To name a few Sabbath rules:

No filtering undrinkable water to make it drinkable.

No picking small bones from fish.

No baking, cooking, or frying of food.

Don't throw an object in the air with one hand and catch it with the other because that constitutes work.

No bowling. Seriously. This falls under the prohibitive category of demolition. It is specifically stated by some rabbis that even gutter balls are not acceptable because they are thrown with the intention of demolition.

Do not pickle a radish because that would cause the radish and the salt to work.

Sounds so relaxing.

Of course, most, if not all, of these rules are debatable depending upon who is doing the interpretation of the overarching Sabbath law.

Sabbath was designed for rest and restoration, but just the thought of trying to determine an acceptable form of rest and restoration makes me tired.

Sabbath. What was intended to be beautiful became a burden. What was intended to be about restoration became about restriction. A day reserved for simplicity became defined by complexity.

Could it be that what the Jewish leaders did to the Sabbath, we have done to Sunday? Take a deep breath. I am not making any accusations, simply asking the question. Could it be?

Clearly there is not an exact parallel between the original Sabbath and Sunday as we now know it. And yet they have eerie similarities.

The original Sabbath was a gift, so with Sunday.

Sabbath began as something simple and was made into something incredibly complex, so with Sunday.

The Sabbath experience was intended to be a meaningful expression of their faith, not the core of their faith, so with Sunday.

When I study what the religious leaders did to and with the Sabbath, I wonder if at some level that is exactly what has happened with Sunday. Like Sabbath, Sunday—in the role it was intended to play in our faith—was God's idea, not man's. Unfortunately, sometimes when we get our fingerprints on a masterpiece of God, it becomes something more than it was intended to be, or perhaps something less.

Like sex—a beautiful, captivating, life-giving gift of God. Or so it was intended to be. Not only has mankind put its fingerprints on the gift of sex, but in many cases has smashed it and remade it into something altogether different from what it was meant to be.

Sex, which was intended to be beautiful, and once was, is often now ugly. Very ugly.

Sex, which was intended to be an act of love, is now often an act of lust.

Sex, which was intended to be a dream, has, in some cases, become a worst nightmare.

Put a gift of God into our hands and sometimes intentionally, many times unintentionally, we turn it into something other than what it was intended to be. We destroy it. We taint it. We twist it. Like sex. Like Sabbath. Like Sunday?

Let me cut to the chase, because there is so much more to discuss. Sunday, and all it entails, can be beautiful and restorative and life-giving when we allow it to play the role it was designed to play and to be. Like Sabbath, Sunday was designed for worship and restoration and encouragement; it was designed as an opportunity for us to rekindle our passion for God and for one another. It was a gathering around a meal—not just any meal, but Communion.

There is no issue with Sunday, just like there is no issue with Sabbath. The issue is when we allow a gift of God to be something more or something less than it was intended to be.

I wonder if God ever experiences déjà vu?

⌐ Reflection/Discussion ⌐

1. Do you agree that in some cases Sunday has become more than it was intended to be? If so, why? If not, why not?

2. Talk about ways to keep Sunday sacred without allowing it to become about rules and regulations.

3. We can easily look back twenty centuries and see how some people lost perspective in regard to Sabbath. When people look back on this generation of Christianity, what do you think people will say about our perspective toward Sunday? Will they say we placed too much emphasis on Sunday? Too little? Will they say we took Sunday too seriously? Not seriously enough? Discuss.

⌐ Prayer ⌐

Father, thank you for the gift of Sunday. Sunday was intended to be a time of restoration, celebration, and worship. May it be nothing more and nothing less in our lives. Teach us ways to keep Sunday sacred in our lives, even if it requires significant changes. Forgive us for the times when we have allowed Sunday to become something more or less than it was intended to be. God, you are the giver of all good gifts, so again, thank you for the beauty and joy of Sunday worship gatherings. In Jesus' name.

5

Lost in Translation

Before you can treat an epidemic there must be a proper diagnosis. We have done that, in part. Indeed, we have discovered, and hopefully acknowledged, that at some level many of us have settled for a faith that is Sunday-centric in nature. However, perhaps our gravitation toward a Sunday faith is just a symptom of our true struggle.

If I were a doctor, my diagnosis would conclude that the reason so many of us struggle with being Sunday Christians is because we have not fully understood the invitation Jesus has given us. More precisely, the invitation has gotten lost in translation.

I don't know about you, but I love to eavesdrop. Often I will be at a restaurant with my wife, and I will miss what she says because I am so busy listening to the conversation behind me, or next to me, or ten tables away if I have a good enough angle to read their lips. You can learn a lot by eavesdropping. If you listen in on certain spiritual discussions—and by "discussions" I mean preaching and teaching that is being done by certain superstar personalities—you just might get the impression that following Jesus is easy.

Correction: Not *might*. You would.

The truth is, following Jesus is simple, but it is certainly not easy.

Jesus said, "If any of you want to be my followers . . . you must take up your cross each day and follow me" (Luke 9:23 CEV).

Pick up a cross. Daily. And follow.

See what I mean? Simple. Not easy.

Unfortunately, Jesus' statement doesn't carry as much shock value now as it once did. We have cleaned up the cross and made it shiny. For us the cross is a decoration, or a piece of jewelry, or an image in a stained-glass window. Now the cross seems harmless. In the first century it was not. The cross was a brutal means of execution. One writer suggested that in the first century if someone wore a cross necklace, it would be like someone wearing an electric-chair necklace now. Doing so would seem vile, inhumane, sick, wicked, and heinous. Those words are all synonyms for *cross*. Not really. But they should be.

In the first century, the cross was something everyone had seen—not hanging on the wall of a church, but with someone hanging on it. History says there were times when thousands of crosses would be lined up along the road, and there was no vacancy. The crosses in action served as a blunt warning: Do not rebel, or else.

When we talk about carrying our cross now, we often do so in reference to a difficult stepmom, or a dead-end job, or the common cold, or a hangnail.

The idea of carrying a cross has gotten lost in translation. Not linguistically, but culturally.

Carrying a cross in the first century meant one thing: you were a dead person walking. You were going to be tied to or nailed to the cross, and the question was not whether or not you would survive, but how long it would take for you to die.

Respected pastor and writer A. W. Tozer said it like this:

The cross operates by destroying one established pattern, the victim's, and creating another pattern, its own. Thus it always has its way. It wins by defeating its opponent and imposing its will upon him. It always dominates. It never comprises, never dickers nor confers, never surrenders a point for the sake of peace. It cares not for peace; it cares only to end its opposition as soon as possible.[1]

Now you can see why, when Jesus invited people to pick up a cross and follow him, so few accepted the offer. When completely understood, Jesus' offer is not one people are quick to sign up for.

It is not an invitation into a life of excess or guaranteed success, or a life void of suffering, struggle, or strife. In fact, Jesus doesn't invite us to live but to die. Seems a bit morbid, don't you think? And this is the same Jesus who said, "I came so that everyone would have life, and have it in its fullest" (John 10:10 CEV).

Which is it? What is Jesus inviting us to? To live or to die? Yes. Both.

Jesus knew that to live you first have to die.

Huh?

This seems illogical to us, but it fits nicely into Jesus' upsidedown kingdom theology. If you want to be first, you have to be last. If you want to be free, be a slave. If you want to live, first you have to die. Whether it seems rational or not, this is the invitation Jesus extends to anyone who would follow him: Die so that you may live.

The invitation to die is not about our flesh and bones, it is about our hearts and minds and souls. Every moment of every day we are dying physically, but the invitation to carry a cross is about dying spiritually. The Bible explains that we have this

1. A. W. Tozer, *The Root of the Righteous* (Camp Hill, PA: WingSpread Publishers, 2007), 68.

monster living just underneath the surface of our skin called "the sinful nature." Our flesh, by its very nature, has an insatiable appetite for evil, for immorality, for self-indulgence of every kind, for sin.

It has not always been this way. In the Old Testament, the first two chapters of Genesis describe a time when sin had not yet snuck in through the back door of creation. It was a short time, but the time before sin was . . .

Beautiful.

Innocent.

Pure.

Holy.

Those first few pages of the Bible tell a tale of love and intimacy, not just between man and woman, but more so between mankind and God, between Creator and creation.

But not for long.

The enemy—the fallen angel, the devil, the snake—showed up and told Eve a story about God. But it was a lie. His stories always are; deception is the only language he knows. The serpent told Eve that if she would just take one bite of that fruit she would be like God. In other words, she would no longer need God; she would become her own god. The lie sounded too good to be true—it was; they always are—but she believed it.

One bite. That is all it took. Then . . .

Pride.

Envy.

Jealousy.

Abuse.

Hate.

Anger.

Lust.

Sin crashed through the door and invaded the world. God's paradise became Satan's playground. And sin did not come in alone; death followed. Death always follows sin. Everywhere. Every time.

Romans 6:23 says, "The wages of sin is death." Death follows sin. The vicious cycle of sin had a death grip on this world until the cross. The cross of Christ. Jesus was not the first man to die on a cross—tens of thousands had died the same way before, but every one of them stayed in the grave. Jesus did not. On the third morning he walked out of his own grave alive.

On Sunday.

Before Jesus, life ended in death. But because of Jesus, now death ends in life—for those who believe and follow in his footsteps.

Dressing up Jesus' invitation a bit would make it more enticing, but it is impossible to do so with a cross. A cross kills. A cross conquers. A cross overwhelms. A cross wins. Always. The invitation to carry a cross is nothing less than an invitation to die daily. It is a call to put to death the desires of our flesh, to ignore the whispers of temptation, to turn away from the allure of instant gratification in a million different ways. Carrying a cross is not comfortable, it is not convenient, it is not easy, but it is necessary to live.

I suppose I can understand why so many Bible teachers and preachers gravitate toward a much more comfortable message. I mean, if you want to do stadium tours and book signings and television broadcasts, you'd better pick a different slogan than "die daily." Share that message and a crowd of thousands will quickly become a handful. Just ask Jesus. A few will remain, but only a very few.

Jesus said there is a narrow road that leads to life, and only a few find it (Matthew 7:14). That narrow road is the road less traveled, and for good reason. Instead of walking down it, stumbling is all you can muster because of the weight of the cross on your back. Jesus knows how much that cross weighs.

A certain man from Cyrene, Simon, the father of Alexander and Rufus, was passing by on his way in from the country, and they forced him to carry the cross. They brought Jesus to the place called Golgotha (which means "the place of the skull"). Then they offered him wine mixed with myrrh, but he did not take it. And they crucified him.

Mark 15:21–24

In a healthy condition, Jesus could have carried the cross on his own, but as he began to stumble down the narrow path of Jerusalem's Via Dolorosa, he had already been beaten to the very edge of death. So Simon carried the cross. But even Simon would have stumbled; crosses are heavy.

Jesus knew the burden of the cross, and yet he said, "Take up [your] cross" (Luke 9:23).

It is only when we accept his invitation to die that we can also accept his invitation to live. Not just life as we know it, but the eternal kind that starts here and now but stretches into the then and there. It is not a life that can be reduced to or measured in days, or weeks, or years. It is a kind of life that is no respecter of days. It is the same on Tuesday and Thursday and Sunday.

A life like this makes anyone and everyone around you aware that you are a passionate follower of Jesus. There would be no other way to explain the way you live.

Even if Sunday didn't exist.

┌─ Reflection/Discussion ─┘

1. When you hear the phrase "take up your cross and follow me," what image or idea comes to mind? How does that invitation apply to your life?

2. In practical terms, what would it look like to truly die to yourself?

3. As you identify changes that need to take place to really die to yourself, determine what hinders you from making some of the changes. Pride? Inconvenience? Fear? Trust?

⌐ Prayer ⌐

Father, remind me every day that I must die to myself. Help me to choose your desires over my own, but also teach me to align my desires with yours. I know that following you will not always be easy; in fact at times it will be painful, but give me the strength to do so. Thank you for carrying the cross that was rightfully mine. In Jesus' name.

Intermission

What you are going to find in the next section is a portrait. Not a painting or sketch or drawing, but nonetheless, a portrait. It is a portrait of the life—the real life—I have been alluding to.

Undoubtedly my word portrait will leave much to be desired. I might as well try to re-create the statue of David with my sons' Play-Doh. But if nothing else, this portrait will serve as a shadow, or perhaps an outline, of the life to which we have been called to live.

If you conducted a man-on-the-street interview and asked people to use words to describe church, you would likely end up with a list like this:

Tame
Stingy
Predictable
Nice
Safe
Boring
Careful

Sadly, these words do describe some churches today, but not the first church, not Jesus' church. Tame, stingy, predictable, nice, safe, boring, careful churches do not get accused of turning the world upside down. Maybe that's why the church today is rarely accused of turning the world upside down.

If you studied the book of Acts, you would have to come up with a very different list of words to describe the church. And when I say the church, I mean a people, not a place. Words like:

Unbridled

Daring

Rebellious

Risky

Relentless

Scandalous

Mad

I suppose I have some explaining to do. I'll keep writing. You keep reading.

Part Two

A Portrait of **real** Life

6

Unbridled

I live in Kentucky. Our country may be the land of the free, but this state is the land of the horses. They call it the Bluegrass State, but I have yet to see a single blade of blue grass; all I see are white fences and horses. A lot of horses. I think if they counted the horses, our state would be awarded another U.S. Representative or two. Horses, horses, everywhere are horses. And every year, Churchill Downs, in Louisville, hosts the world-famous Kentucky Derby.

Now, I have only ridden a horse once in my lifetime, and my knowledge about them is as limited as my riding experience. I know they have four feet, or hoofs (I'm not sure), and are measured in hands, which makes no sense to me. Oh yeah, and they wear shoes. I also know that horses often wear a bridle attached to reins so the rider can control the movement, speed, and direction of the horse.

To be bridled is to be contained, controlled, restrained, limited.

To be unbridled is to be uncontained, uncontrolled, unrestrained, unlimited.

If the average person were asked to choose one of these words—bridled or unbridled—to describe the followers of Christ they know, I am afraid more often than not they would choose bridled.

Contained.

Controlled.

Restrained.

Limited.

My guess is that some followers of Christ would proudly claim such adjectives. However, the first Christians, in the first church, would have never been described by such terms. That doesn't mean they were not obedient followers of Christ, because they were. It doesn't mean there was no discipline in their lives, because there was. It *does* mean they lived life unbridled.

They could not be contained; they could not be controlled; they could not be restrained; and they could not be limited. They were generous with God and with one another.

As you study through the pages of Acts, you find evidence of a generosity that was . . .

Lavish.

Extravagant.

Excessive.

Prolific.

Unbridled.

Acts 4:32 says, "All the believers were one in heart and mind. No one claimed that any of his possessions was his own, but they shared everything they had."

They didn't share some things. Or a lot of things. Or most things. But everything. With everyone.

We have all heard the saying "There is no *I* in team." The first believers' motto seems to have been "There is no *my* in church." No one claimed any possessions as his or her own. Not my car, not my house, not my bank account, not my clothes. Not *my*, but *our*.

Everything is ours. Let's be honest, that may sound inspiring, but at the same time we can start quietly asking a long line of questions in our minds.

What if I let "them" live in my house and their kids do damage? What if I let them borrow my car and it comes back wrecked? What if I lend them some of my money and they never pay it back? What if they wear my clothes and ruin them with a stain, or I never get them back?

Articulating such a list of questions was not difficult for me, because I have asked them. And I am probably not the only one. Right? But did you notice the inherent problems with all of the questions?

My. My. My. My. As responsible as those questions may seem, they would no longer exist if the word *my* was deleted from the dictionary and replaced with *our*.

Does that mean we shouldn't take good care of things? Does it mean we should be flippant with money? Does it mean we should be all right when things are abused? No. It just means we should not allow orbiting in a galaxy of unanswerable questions to pose as responsible reasons for not being generous with others.

I know. I know. This all sounds a bit too socialistic for comfort. I get it. You deal with thoughts like these too long and you start thinking about communes and purple Kool-Aid and white tennis shoes. But we are not talking about a cult or a commune. We are not even talking about capitalism or socialism. We are talking about a community—a Christ-centered community called the church. And there is no *my* in church.

There were no needy persons among them.

Acts 4:34

Can you imagine that? Think about the place you worship, or more so, the people you worship with. Think of their names and faces and stories. You likely know a small portion of the people who make up your local church. So take some time to write down the physical needs that are represented just within the circle of people you know. Really. Stop for a moment and make a list.

I don't know the people you know, but I know people you don't, and I'll bet the list of needs we would come up with would be much the same.

Missed mortgage payments.

Medical bills.

Car repairs.

Court fees.

Child support.

Service dog for an autistic child.

The list could go on and on and on.

In my setting, I know of more needs than I could ever articulate, and honestly, I am glad I do not know more because it gets to be overwhelming. And depressing. At times I have grown numb because there are so many needs.

Now read again what Acts 4:34 says about the first church:

There were no needy persons among them.

Not figuratively. Literally. No unpaid bills. No empty food pantries. No medical needs going unmet. No needs. None. No needy persons among them. How?

For from time to time those who owned lands or houses sold them, brought the money from the sales and put it at the apostles' feet, and it was distributed to anyone who had need.

Joseph, a Levite from Cyprus, whom the apostles called Barnabas (which means "son of encouragement"), sold a field he owned and brought the money and put it at the apostles' feet.

Acts 4:34–37

Selling lands.

Selling houses.

Giving the money to the church to be distributed to those in need.

Not just once. From time to time.

In the church I lead, there have been some isolated incidents of lands-and-houses-type generosity. Recently we had a married couple donate a house—a nice house—to the church with no strings attached.

Last year I became aware of a single mother who was doing her very best to try to make ends meet for her family. She was employed but lacked reliable transportation, which was threatening her ability to work. The director of our benevolence fund asked what I thought we could do to provide her a car. At first I thought, *No way. How could we do that?* But then my second thought was a better one (in my case it usually is). I decided I would give our congregation an opportunity to meet the need. So that next Sunday at the end of our worship service I announced the need, and yes, I tugged on the heartstrings a bit. "Who is going to meet the need? Who is going to donate a car? Who is going to be the church?" Then, before I walked off the platform, I said, "I cannot wait to celebrate together next weekend when I share about the car that has been donated." Quite the dangerous statement to make in front of fifteen hundred people. *What if no one comes through?* I should have taken a second thought before I spoke. But I didn't.

That week we didn't get a car donated.

We received four.

Four nice, safe, drivable cars. The biggest challenge for our benevolence team was all the detail work to get them tagged and insured.

Unbridled generosity. I have experienced it, I have seen it, and it is beautiful. Actually, it is stunning, because that type of generosity is so rare.

We have said as followers of Jesus that when it comes to money and possessions, it is not mine but ours. And that is true. Kind of. Because it is not even really ours. It is God's. Everything.

Besides fear, I continue to find that the biggest hindrance to a life of generosity—both to one another and to God—is not understanding the issue of ownership. Psalm 24:1 says, "The earth is the LORD's, and everything in it, the world, and all who live in it."

Nothing is ours. Everything is his. His stars. His oceans. His mountains. His animals. His sun. His moon. His plains and valleys. His forests and jungles. Every grain of sand, every mote of dust.

His.

All of it. And yet God shares. With us. With everyone. With the righteous and the unrighteous.

The title for your house has your name on it, but it is his. So is your neighbor's house.

The extra car you saved up to buy, that's his too.

Your clothes . . . are his.

Your food . . . is his.

Your bank account. Yep. His.

And your 401k . . .

And your stock portfolio. It's all his.

Look in front of you, behind you, on top of you, under you, and all around you. It is all his, and he is sharing it with you. So how does that sound? Socialistic? Or generous?

I have thrown around the word *socialistic* a bit, and because it is a sticky word, let me offer some clarity. There is a significant difference between true socialism and living in the midst of a Christ-centered community marked by unbridled generosity.

One is forced, the other is chosen. One is motivated by obligation, the other is motivated by love.

God's generosity is motivated by love, but maybe the best word to describe God's generosity is . . .

Unbridled.

How would you describe your lifestyle of generosity to others and to God?

Contained?

Restrained?

Limited?

Or, unbridled?

Honestly.

To be clear, it is possible to donate even something valuable and not be generous; it all depends on the motivation. So the real question is not whether or not you have sold a house or a piece of land to help meet the needs of others, but would you?

Most of us would like to answer with a resounding yes, and then there are those who would actually do it. You would hire a Realtor. Schedule open houses. Create a posting on Craigslist. Put up a sign. You would sell your home.

But like the saying goes, "You really don't know what you would do until faced with the decision." Not sure if that is a saying or not, but I guess it is now. Still, I don't think there is much benefit in dealing with what-if scenarios anyway, so let's get intensely practical.

Do you have an empty room in your house? Or rooms?

Statistics say most of us do. My wife and I do. Several times we have discussed inviting a particular person or family to live in our home, and in most scenarios we are able to come up with a list of reasons why it wouldn't be the best fit, or how it would be inconvenient. Or we find ourselves getting lost in questions like "Do we put a time frame on the arrangement?" "What if it doesn't work out?" "What if it's awkward?" And so in the midst of the what-if questions, the conversation usually fades and the rooms sit empty.

Now, in fairness, there have been times we have offered our home, and the invitees have declined for a variety of reasons. Still, the fact remains that we have a large room on the second floor of our home that is empty.

Do you?

This is not an indictment; it is an opportunity for honest reflection.

Obviously the issue of generosity is not just about homes and lands and rooms. It is also about cars and meals and rides and gas money and school supplies and medicine and . . . the list could go on forever. There is something glamorous about selling something to meet the needs of others, but truthfully, a life of unbridled generosity is more often mundane and ordinary. You will find yourself putting extra groceries in the cart, more gas in the car, fresh sheets on a spare bed, and additional presents under the tree.

No matter its form, generosity creates opportunities for needs to be met. And not just physical needs, spiritual needs too.

> With great power the apostles continued to testify to the resurrection of the Lord Jesus. And God's grace was so powerfully at work in them all. . . .
>
> Acts 4:33

This oft-overlooked verse seems to show a connection between generosity and the spread of the gospel. Is it possible that in the midst of selling lands and homes so that every need could be met, a few people in the secular world took notice?

What kind of impact would be made in your neighborhood, if suddenly there was a FOR SALE sign in front of your house? The neighbors would ask, "Have you been transferred with work?" "Have you been forced to foreclose because of the economy?" "Are you getting divorced?" "Do you just want new neighbors?"

With the right level of humility, you would be able to answer, "No, I am selling so I can use the money to meet the needs of others." It isn't hard to predict the next question: "Why?" And then you could explain that your generosity is because you have been the recipient of such generosity. Perhaps the next question would be, "From whom?" And then . . .

I'll stop there. I think you see how the story would quickly make its way to Jesus, especially if this kind of generosity was not just an isolated event but part of a pattern that was easily identified within the Christian community.

Radio news commentator Paul Harvey is dead now, but I was a big fan of his. He was famous for the line: "And now, the rest of the story . . ."

Earlier I told you how we asked for a car to be donated and we received four. One of the cars went to Julia (not her real name), a single mother of three, struggling to make ends meet, living in a trailer with no electricity, and, oh, by the way, battling an aggressive form of cancer.

Well, as sad as it may sound, my excitement over the donated car faded quickly in the midst of busyness and other ministry demands, and I didn't give it another thought. Until about six weeks later.

I received a call that there was someone who wanted to be baptized on a Monday evening at church, and the person wanted to know if I would do the baptism. "Sure," I said. "Who is it?"

Julia.

I will never forget that night as I stood backstage with Julia, preparing to baptize her. I had heard bits and pieces of her story, but I wanted to hear it from her.

Julia told me about the difficulty of raising three children while struggling to make ends meet, the recurring bouts with cancer and the nauseating chemotherapy that she had endured. She explained how the day before she received the donated car she had been riding home on a city bus from her chemotherapy treatment and had to get off at a random bus stop because she was so sick from the treatment that she couldn't stop vomiting.

When I asked what had led her to surrender her life to Jesus, Julia answered without hesitation: "I realized God is on my side."

One person donated an extra car to a single mother.

A single mother realized God was on her side.

That is the rest of the story. For now.

Because the story of unbridled generosity is still being written; there are new chapters every day.

Men, women, and children who are living lives surrendered to the Holy Spirit are doing the writing. They come in all shapes, sizes, and colors. They are from every corner of the globe, and they live in cities and suburbs and rural areas. They are blue-collar workers and white-collar workers. They are vocational ministers and lay leaders and silent servants.

They—no matter who they are or where they are from—are all writing the same story: the story of unbridled generosity.

Are you one of them?

If not, pick up a pen and start writing.

⌐ Reflection/Discussion ⌐

1. Honestly evaluate your own generosity to God and to others. Which word fits best: bridled or unbridled?

2. If you struggle with generosity, what is the true source of your struggle?

3. Brainstorm practical ways you could live a life of unbridled generosity. Some will involve money, but often the greatest opportunities are more about time, talent, and energy. After you develop a list, start weaving these opportunities into daily life.

A few ideas to get you started . . .

- If you have an extra room in the house, talk with the appropriate people about who might need a place to stay.

- If you have an extra car, ask around until you find someone who needs it more than you, then give it away.

- If you know a family who is struggling to afford food, schedule one night a week to take dinner to them.

- Intentionally invest in a widow and share your family with her.

- On your next birthday, use any money you receive to meet a tangible need for a neighbor or co-worker or random stranger.

- And so on . . . This is your chance to dream!

4. Our culture is so different from the first-century world, but how can we re-create a similar pattern of unbridled generosity? Discuss what your church and community would be like if every need was met.

⌐ Prayer ⌐

Father, thank you for all of the incredible gifts you have poured into our lives. Forgive us for the times we have been tight-fisted. Help me to develop a lifestyle of unbridled generosity. As I give generously to you and to others, I pray you will create opportunities for me to give you the glory. In Jesus' name.

7

Daring

When I was sixteen or so, I visited an amusement park with my best friend (actually, he was my only friend) and was mesmerized by a bungee-jumping tower. At the time, bungee jumping was a newfangled idea. After inquiring, it seemed like a good deal: only $75 to put my courage on display for the world to see, or at least the eleven people who happened to be lingering around.

Back then I pretended I was not afraid of anything, but nothing could have been further from the truth. I was afraid of snakes, the dark, cats (yes, seriously), and anyone of normal size who even looked at me wrong. See, at sixteen, I was approximately the size of a ten-year-old. Even though I was a scared little man, I mean boy, I pretended I was not. So without giving a second thought, I paid the money for the ride and began putting on the necessary gear.

As I climbed the tall tower I reviewed in my mind all of the possible jumping options. Backwards. Swan dive. Somersault. Double-somersault. Once on the jumping platform I quickly made my way to the edge and then made the worst mistake possible. I looked down. Suddenly I was no longer considering jumping positions. I was thinking of an exit strategy, but there was none available. The employee very nicely explained that he would count to three and then I would jump—or else he would push. At the count of three I like to say I jumped, but I think I was helped, and there was no somersault; I chose the pencil position. After the initial free fall, which only lasted about one second but felt like an eternity, I suddenly found myself enjoying the experience. I began screaming loudly, which was my attempt to make the whole experience seem like it was child's play.

Finally I was lowered down to the ground and my gear was removed. What I did next must have been the result of a lack of oxygen. I chose to jump again. I couldn't pass it up; the second jump was only $50. After getting the gear back on, I walked up the tower and again considered jumping positions I would take. Backwards. Swan dive. Somersault. Double-somersault. Pencil. You know which one I chose.

That day I walked away $125 poorer but with my chest swelled up, as much as my bird chest could swell up, thinking that I just displayed my lack of fear for the whole world to see.

Actually it was stupidity. Who pays to jump off a tall tower, or anything for that matter, with a bungee cord tied around their feet? Twice?

Me.

Some people try to prove they have courage; other people actually do.

Two of Jesus' first followers, Peter and John, had daring courage.

As Acts 4 begins, we find Peter and John settling into the familiar confines of a prison cell where they will spend the night. I know what you're thinking: Jesus' disciples were a rowdy bunch. Well, yes, they were, but not in this particular instance. They had been arrested for preaching. Again. They couldn't resist sharing the gospel of Jesus, especially when surrounded by a crowd. A crowd had definitely surrounded them this time, and they had been surrounded for good reason.

The day began as an ordinary day. Acts 3:1 says, "One day Peter and John were going up to the temple at the time of prayer—at three in the afternoon." That does not sound like the beginning of a day that is going to end in a jail cell. Typically, those stories begin with phrases like "I was in the wrong place at the wrong time," or "We were only going to have a few," or "He started it." Anyway, you can imagine the reaction Peter and John would get when they began their prison story with "We were on our way to the temple at the time of prayer . . ." People in the crowd would be nudging each other, trying to hide their smirk, thinking, *Sure you were.* But they *really were* on their way to the temple at the time of prayer.

> Now a man who was lame from birth was being carried to the temple gate called Beautiful, where he was put every day to beg from those going into the temple courts. When he saw Peter and John about to enter, he asked them for money. Peter looked straight at him, as did John. Then Peter said, "Look at us!" So the man gave them his attention, expecting to get something from them.
>
> Acts 3:2–5

Still doesn't sound like a crime scene.

> Then Peter said, "Silver or gold I do not have, but what I do have I give you. In the name of Jesus Christ of Nazareth, walk."
>
> Acts 3:6

And he did.

If there is any scene in the Bible that I would want to have watched from a front row seat with a bucket of popcorn, this would be near the top of the list.

This beggar was not suffering from a sprained ankle. He did not have turf toe. He did not have a hangnail on his big toe, which can keep even the biggest man down, or so I hear.

The man was crippled; he had been born that way. His parents couldn't reminisce together as they watched videos of him taking his first step, because he had never taken a first step. He was carried everywhere. Because he was born crippled, his place in life was determined for him. In that day there were no social services, there were no disability checks. If you were born crippled, you were destined to spend your entire life begging.

And he had. All day. Every day. Until the day he met Peter and John.

They said, "In the name of Jesus Christ of Nazareth, walk." And he did.

Can you imagine this man walking for the first time? Perhaps he was a bit wobbly—people, or babies I should say, usually *are* when they take their first step. Maybe he had a hard time keeping his balance. Surely he would have scuffed up his knees, except they were already scarred over from resting on them all day, every day.

Suddenly this crippled man was walking and jumping and skipping to and fro. And everyone was watching. Wouldn't you? The Bible tells us the crowd recognized this as the same man who had sat at the temple gate begging month after month, year after year. They couldn't help but stare. And wonder.

While the man held on to Peter and John, all the people were astonished and came running to them in the place called Solomon's Colonnade.

Acts 3:11

64

The people surrounded Peter and John. Not some of the people. Not most of the people. All the people.

Peter and John only knew how to do one thing when surrounded by people: preach; and so they did. That is when the trouble began.

They might have been fine if they would have preached a warm and fuzzy message about Jesus, the kind that fills up stadiums today, but messages about Jesus being murdered on the cross are not so warm and fuzzy. Especially when you accuse the crowd of committing the murder. That is exactly what Peter did. The CliffsNotes version of the sermon he preached goes like this: "You murdered Jesus. Now repent." That is not the kind of sermon you preach and then stand at the back of the sanctuary and shake the hands of little old women as they leave. Preaching that sermon, especially to Jewish religious leaders in the first century, gets you arrested; and it did.

Now we are back where we began. Peter and John, late at night, sitting in a prison cell.

The next morning they were taken to testify before the Sanhedrin, which was the religious authority of the day. One would think that a night in a cold, damp prison cell would be enough to convince anyone to be a bit less outspoken, just to preserve their own freedom and safety if for no other reason. Perhaps after a night in shackles they would realize that it would be in their best interest to rationalize away the events of the previous day by calling it a big misunderstanding. They could have used the most popular phrase among professional athletes, entertainers, and politicians when they find themselves in a bit of a self-imposed bind: "Our comments were taken out of context." If Peter and John would have taken such an approach, very likely this whole fiasco they were in could have been quickly and quietly resolved; but they didn't.

Acts 4:7 says, "They had Peter and John brought before them and began to question them: 'By what power or what name did you do this?'"

As the story plays out, we are told that Peter, filled with the Holy Spirit, shared the same sermon with the religious leaders as he had the day before with the large crowd. There was no cute introduction, no finely tuned outline, just one clear message: You murdered Jesus, and God raised him from the dead.

Sharing such a bold message about Jesus in the twenty-first century on a street corner in New York City, when and where there are no legal implications at stake, is one thing. Doing so in the early first century while standing before the Sanhedrin is another. The crowd in New York City may be annoyed; the Sanhedrin had the authority to have Peter and John imprisoned, beaten, or worse. For Peter and John, this was not a low-stakes gamble; they were all in. Fortunately for Peter and John, though the Sanhedrin wanted desperately to severely punish them for their behavior, they couldn't decide how to punish them, and so after making harmless threats, they let them go. The Sanhedrin was actually afraid of how the crowds would respond because all the people were praising God for the miracle that had taken place.

Some pretend to have courage, some actually do.

In this whole passage, the most captivating statement comes right after Peter finished his sermon: "When they saw the courage of Peter and John and realized that they were unschooled, ordinary men, they were astonished and took note that these men had been with Jesus" (Acts 4:13).

I find it interesting that what made it apparent to the religious leaders that Peter and John had been with Jesus was not their biblical knowledge, their eloquence, or their physical appearance, but their courage. That may sound surprising until you remember that some of these very same religious leaders would have been present during the trials of Jesus. Not long before they had questioned Peter and John, they had questioned Jesus.

If anyone would have been tempted to buckle under the pressure, or to explain away some of his earlier claims, it would have been Jesus. After all, he knew what was coming. He was not going to be threatened and released the way Peter and John were; he was going to be hung on a cross to die. So when the men asked him if he really was the king of the Jews, he could have backed away from that claim or denied ever saying such a thing. Instead, with death staring him in the face, he simply said, "It is as you say." That night as the religious leaders had Jesus scourged, mocked, and crucified, they could deny him his dignity, and they could deny he was who he claimed to be, but there was one thing they could not deny: his courage.

When Peter and John stared severe punishment in the face and refused to back down or back away from what they knew to be true, when they put their courage on display, it is no wonder the religious leaders took note that they had been with Jesus.

This was not an isolated display of courage from Jesus' followers; it was a lifestyle. In fact, historians suggest that at least ten of Jesus' first followers were killed as a direct result of their commitment to him and to preaching the gospel message about him.

Andrew—crucified

Bartholomew—crucified

James, son of Alphaeus—stoned

James, son of Zebedee—sword

Peter—crucified

Philip—crucified

Thomas—speared

Jude—crucified

Matthew—speared

Simon—crucified

Based on this pattern, it sort of seems that dying for Jesus is a prerequisite to be considered a person of courage. But that is not the case.

There is one thing that requires the same courage as dying for Jesus does.

Living for Jesus.

Daily.

In the good times and the bad.

In sickness and in health.

In poverty and in wealth.

When it is popular and when it is not.

When it is profitable and when it is not.

Living for Jesus daily requires courage. Daring courage.

Ask the woman who is married to an unbelieving spouse. Constantly he mocks her faith, and yet she continues to love and serve him as an expression of her faith in Jesus Christ. For years she has prayed that his heart would soften, and yet there are no signs of that happening. In fact, it seems, if anything, his heart has grown harder. She is not living life alone, but she is working out her salvation alone.

Ask the missionary who is working among an unreached people group. Early in life he committed to spending all of his days working among those people. At first it seemed like a thrill, but now twenty years into his work, there is still not even one conversion. He has been tempted to quit, yet he presses on because he is convinced the light is about to pierce the darkness.

Ask the middle-aged Christian man who is diagnosed with a debilitating terminal disease. One month he was running several miles every day, the next he is struggling to tie his own shoes. The family had always depended on him for everything, now he depends on them for everything, even help to use the restroom.

The truth is, you likely don't need to ask anyone about the courage required to live for Jesus daily. If you are following Jesus, you already know. Most of us will not be asked to die for Jesus, but we are all called to live for Jesus. Daily.

It takes courage to do so. What does that look like in your life? To do an honest courage evaluation in our lives, it may be helpful to answer a list of questions like these:

How do you respond to the college professor who consistently and dogmatically claims God is not real? Or do you?

How are you dealing with the terminal condition you are experiencing?

How are you responding to your new, uninvited, unexpected status of being unemployed?

How do you respond to temptation even when no one is looking?

What do you do when the circumstances of this life beat you up, throw you down, and wear you out?

These are moments of life—and there are so many others like them—when our courage or lack thereof is exposed. It is easy to study Acts 3 and 4 and immediately conclude that even in the face of severe punishment, perhaps even death, we would respond the way Peter and John did. Really? Even if so, the real test of our courage is not how we would theoretically respond in a situation we will most likely never face, but how we are responding in the daily circumstances we are facing.

First Corinthians 16:13 says, "Be on your guard; stand firm in the faith; be courageous; be strong."

Some people pretend to have courage; others actually do.

Followers of Jesus don't have to pretend.

⌐ Reflection/Discussion ⌐

1. Tell your group about a time when you tried something silly in order to prove your courage. (People will not make fun of you . . . to your face.)

2. Courage is not one of the first attributes we think about in regard to Jesus-followers, but it is a necessary one. Think about circumstances of life that require great courage, especially for Christians.

3. In the circumstances you came up with, do you tend to respond courageously? If not, why not?

⌐ Prayer ⌐

Father, there are some circumstances of this life that require an incredible amount of courage. I ask that you would give me the courage I need when and where I need it. Your Holy Spirit is my source of courage, so remind me not to rely on myself, or I will end up backing down when I need to stand up. I pray that people will see you at work in me because of my courage in the midst of difficult circumstances. In Jesus' name.

8

Rebellious

I attended Ozark Christian College in Joplin, Missouri, for years, many years. Suffice it to say, I squeezed a four-year degree into seven years. Barely. The summer after my second junior year, I served on an Ozark Camp Team. A Camp Team was typically made up of two girls and two guys, and you spent the summer—all summer—traveling and serving at one junior/senior high camp after another. It's not as bad as it sounds. What's not to like about spending ten weeks with people who do not wear deodorant, change their clothes, or brush their teeth?

As you can imagine, it was a long summer. When we pulled into the final campground, I was already mentally unplugged and ready to go home, sleep in, and eat edible food again. I was dreading the week, but it was a week that changed my life. Actually, it was someone I met who changed my life.

Blake. I wish you knew him.

The first day, I was sitting in the cafeteria for lunch, when the door opened and Blake came in. Rolled in. His mother was pushing his wheelchair, and she found the one open spot in the room, next to me. I tried to exchange pleasantries, but Blake didn't reciprocate. He wasn't able to do so. He couldn't talk, or at least the sounds he made weren't understandable to anyone except his mother. Blake was severely physically and mentally disabled, unable to control the movement of his head, arms, or legs. He was imprisoned in his own body. I soon learned, however, that his body may have been sick, but his soul was well. Very well.

Though communication was difficult, I was able to develop a meaningful relationship with Blake that week. I quickly realized we shared some passions in life, especially two.

Jesus and chocolate milk.

Every meal, Blake would squeal with delight as he drank multiple cartons of chocolate milk. His mother would pour the milk into his mouth, much of it overflowing onto his shirt and pants. But it didn't matter. Blake loved every minute of it, or should I say, every ounce. Each carton was as great as the last. As the week progressed, Blake's mother gave me some insight into his life, as well as his hopes and dreams. Most kids Blake's age dream dreams of success and fame and wealth. Blake's dream? To ride in the church van. Because of his disability, he always had to ride in his mother's car, following the church van. So when the youth group loaded up to go to church camp, everyone picked their spot in the van, everyone except for Blake. Every year.

I will never forget the last day of camp. Several of us gathered around Blake in his wheelchair, and with his mother's permission, we gently picked him up and placed him in the front seat of the van. As we did, he smiled uncontrollably and squealed at a deafening level.

My thoughts still gravitate to Blake now and then and the seeming limitations he faced. He would never go on a date, swim in a pool, drive a car, feed himself, take a shower on his own, get married, or have kids. Some would say Blake's life was empty, but I tell you, his life was full . . . of joy, a joy not contained by or concerned with life's circumstances. Blake's was a *rebellious joy.*

Real joy always is.

If you and I played a game of word association and I asked what came to your mind when I said "rebellious," you might mention "criminal," or "convict," or the name of your favorite two-year-old. Yes, *rebellious* is usually cast in a negative light, but its definition—"resisting management"—isn't necessarily negative. *Rebellious* is also not often used as an adjective for joy, mainly because joy is misunderstood.

Almost universally we confuse happiness with joy. At times they do overlap, but not always. It is interesting that in the Galatians 5 passage where the fruit of the Spirit are articulated, *joy* is there but *happiness* is nowhere to be found.

The thing is, happiness is attainable, but it is never sustainable. And here is why: Happiness is dependent on circumstances. When the housing market is surging, the unemployment rate is low, bonuses are being given, vacations are being taken, new cars are being purchased, and awards are being won, the happiness quotient in your life is likely to be sky high. But when the bubble bursts, the pink slip shows up, the check-engine light in your high-mileage car is on, and no one is noticing you or your work, happiness disappears.

Not only is joy independent of human circumstances, it often rebels against human circumstances. Joy shows up in places where happiness never would. Like prison.

In Acts 16 we find the apostle Paul in prison. Again. This time he had been jailed for preaching the gospel of Christ. Just like every other time. I know, shame on him.

During college I spent a lot of time in prison. No, not serving time, but doing ministry. The Missouri State Penitentiary had some nice amenities, far more than the Bible-college dorm room I lived in; for example, cable TV, or any TV for that matter. I do not want to make light of people who spend months or years living in prison, but the truth is, there are some prison privileges and amenities now that didn't exist in the first century, including weight rooms, Ping-Pong tables, computers, libraries, and did I mention cable TV?

So when Acts 16 says Paul was in prison, it was a first-century prison, not a retreat center. Living in a cell. Chains. Hunger. Thirst. Paul had given up everything to follow after Jesus—his career, his accomplishments, his prestigious religious position. As a result, he found himself in a prison. Not only was Paul in prison, but the Bible tells us he had been flogged before he was locked away. Then his feet were placed in stocks and he was locked up. So it would be easy to understand if Paul sat in the prison cell with his head bowed, not praying but pouting.

Yet Acts 16:25 says, "About midnight Paul and Silas were praying and singing hymns to God, and the other prisoners were listening to them." Singing in prison. Was Paul happy? Absolutely not. Was he joyful? Absolutely.

Joy is not of this world; in fact, it is in a sense otherworldly. Not in an extraterrestrial kind of way, but otherworldly nonetheless. See, joy is not manufactured or produced by us, but by God. In us.

Just a bit ago we talked about how joy is mentioned as being fruit of the Holy Spirit. In the greater context of Galatians 5, the apostle Paul builds the case that our freedom found in Christ will be used to live one way or another—either fulfilling every desire of our flesh, or fulfilling the desires of the Holy Spirit of God who lives in us. There is this battle raging inside of us every moment of every day. Paul explained the conflict by saying, "I do not understand what I do. For what I want to do I do not do, but what I hate I do" (Romans 7:15). The battle between our flesh and the Spirit will continue until we take our last breath in this life, but here is what we must not forget: We are not innocent bystanders. Though we will be tugged back and forth by the power of temptation and the sway of the Holy Spirit, ultimately we choose how we live. When we willingly surrender ourselves—all of ourselves to him—then the fruit of the Spirit begins to grow and flourish in our lives.

Like joy. We cannot produce it, or manufacture it, but we can choose it by surrendering ourselves to the will and the way of the Holy Spirit of God. (If only it were that easy, right?) That is the way fruit is produced, but if simply knowing this truth translated into abundant fruit in our lives, all of us would produce enough fruit to open up a corner store in New York City. There must be something more that allowed Paul to sing in prison; I think there was.

Paul believed God's promises are true.

In 2 Corinthians 12, Paul explains that three times he asked God to remove a thorn in his flesh. Biblical scholars have debated long about what Paul was alluding to. Some have suggested poor eyesight, others a speech impediment, and still others that perhaps Paul suffered from epilepsy. The specifics of his condition really don't matter at this point. What matters is how he handled the situation.

Paul prayed. Repeatedly.

Three times he asked the Lord to remove the thorn in his flesh, and God said no. Well, he didn't use the word *no*, but his answer was no. God's actual words were: "My grace is sufficient for you, for my power is made perfect in your weakness" (v. 9).

I think many of us tend to categorize a *no* from God as an unanswered prayer. But it is not. It may not be what we were looking for, but it is an answer that sometimes, maybe even often, God gives to the most sincere prayers. Remember in the garden of Gethsemane, when Jesus prayed for the Father to take the cup of suffering from him? God said no. When we get a no, we are in good company.

For Paul, the no included a reason. Again, God said, "My grace is sufficient for you, for my power is made perfect in weakness." The suffering, the discomfort, the inconvenience, the thorn was necessary for God's strength to be fully seen and experienced. See, in the absence of suffering, discomfort, or inconvenience, we tend to rely on our own strength, which is puny.

Don't miss this. God's response to Paul was not just a reason, it was a promise. God did not say, "My grace might be sufficient for you, for my power might be made perfect in your weakness."

Not might be, but *is.*

God responded to Paul with a fact. A reason. A promise.

And Paul was able and willing to endure pain, suffering, even the thorn in his flesh—whatever it might have been—because he knew that in the midst of it God's power was being made perfect and God's grace was enough. In Paul's words: "That is why, for Christ's sake, I delight in weaknesses, in insults, in hardships, in persecutions, in difficulties" (v. 10).

Paul was convinced God's promises are true. Are you?

All throughout Scripture, there are woven promises of God. Not just to someone, but to *us.* These are just a few:

Jesus said, "Come to me all who are weary and burdened, and I will give you rest."

Matthew 11:28

Jesus said, "My Father's house has many rooms; if that were not so, would I have told you that I am going there to prepare a place for you? And if I go and prepare a place for you, I will come back and take you to be with me that you also may be where I am."

John 14:2–3

Jesus said, "I will be with you always, even until the end of the world."

Matthew 28:20 CEV

Not might be, *will be.*

It is not enough to say we believe God's promises; we must live by them. Paul did. And he did not choose joy in the midst of suffering because it was enjoyable, but because he believed God's grace was sufficient. When he was whipped, stripped, and left for dead, God was strong. For Paul, that was reason to choose joy.

But as you study Paul's life and writings, you find another reason as well.

Paul knew his suffering was not in vain.

It seems obvious that Paul was a sports fan. Really. If he lived today, he would have ESPN, ESPN 2 and ESPNews. He is a man after my own heart, or perhaps I am a man after his. Either way, we know Paul was keenly aware of the athletic goings-on around him because he often used sports imagery in his writings:

Do you not know that in a race all the runners run, but only one gets the prize? Run in such a way as to get the prize. Everyone who competes in the games goes into strict training. They do it to get a crown that will not last, but we do it to get a crown that will last forever.

1 Corinthians 9:24–25

Brothers and sisters, I do not consider myself yet to have taken hold of it. But one thing I do: Forgetting what is behind, and straining toward what is ahead, I press on toward the goal to win the prize for which God has called me heavenward in Christ Jesus.

Philippians 3:13–14

Paul knew there was a prize awaiting him—and us. Not a plastic bowling trophy that is destined to collect dust and hold down papers, but a crown of life that will never wither, fade, or die.

Paul knew well the struggles of the here and now but filled his mind with thoughts of the there and then. I don't know for sure what it all means—truthfully, I don't think anyone does—but in his second letter to the Corinthians, Paul makes allusions to the fact that he was given a glimpse of the life to come:

> I know a man in Christ who fourteen years ago was caught up to the third heaven. Whether it was in the body or out of the body I do not know—God knows. And I know that this man—whether in the body or apart from the body I do not know, but God knows—was caught up to paradise. He heard inexpressible things, things that man is not permitted to tell.
>
> 2 Corinthians 12:2–4

Have you ever wanted to share something so badly but were not able to? And so you did everything you could to communicate without actually sharing it? Sounds like that is what Paul is doing. As you read the language he used—"I know a man in Christ who . . ."—one cannot help but conclude that man was the same one who would stare back at Paul when he looked in a mirror. Again, I cannot prove that, but if so, then Paul had experienced a taste of paradise. And apparently that momentary experience of coming perfection in the next life allowed him to endure the realities of imperfection in this life. With joy.

The joy that the Holy Spirit gives—and the joy Paul had—rebels against any and every circumstance of this life. Holy Spirit joy endures the here and now but swells with anticipation for the there and then. A lifestyle saturated with Holy Spirit joy causes people to look and listen. Even in prison.

. . . and the other prisoners were listening to them.

Acts 16:25

So how about us? Is that the kind of joy we have? A joy that is rebellious? A joy that rebels against any and all circumstances of this life? If you are like me, then the answer is sometimes, which means the answer is really no.

We all have moments when joy comes easily. Holding a new baby in our arms. Finally holding the diploma. Getting a raise. Saying "I do." Lying on the beach. Joy comes easy in those moments. But there are so many other moments of life when it seems difficult if not impossible to muster up any joy. When the doctor says there is no heartbeat. Standing next to a freshly dug grave. Reading the Dear John note. Getting the pink slip in the mail. Finding the foreclosure notice on the door. When the test results come back negative, or positive.

In these moments it is easier to scream than to sing. In these moments, and so many others like them, joy seems elusive.

Honestly, for most of us, a lack of desire is not the issue. Perhaps the real issue is the way we try to attain a sustainable joy. Joy is much like the rest of the fruit of the Holy Spirit in this way. When we notice an absence in our lives, our instinct is to try to manufacture it on our own.

The key word is *try*. If the trying we have done hasn't developed the fruit we desire in our lives, the natural response is to try harder. And so we do our best. In a sense we try as hard as we can to try harder.

Do you see the futility in our instinctive response? Trying harder sounds noble, it seems respectable, yet it is futile. The joy factor in your life and mine will never be a result of working hard; it will always be the natural by-product of living a life surrendered to the will and way of the Holy Spirit. And yet for most of us, our next question is, "What do I need to do to live a life surrendered to the Holy Spirit?"

In other words, what can I work hard at? So we are back to the beginning of the vicious cycle. Human effort.

Living a life surrendered to the will and the way of the Holy Spirit is not so much about doing as about being.

Calm.

Still.

Quiet.

Then, you can hear the voice of the Holy Spirit.

Whispering.

Speaking.

Shouting.

When you can regularly hear the voice of the Holy Spirit whispering, speaking, shouting about the there and then, you are able to live—really live—in the here and now.

With joy.

My finest memory from that last week of camp happened on Thursday night. If you have experienced the church-camp scene, you know Thursday night is the night where there is weeping and gnashing of teeth. Not so much the gnashing, but definitely the weeping. When the speaker closes the final message and the invitation is given, it seems like every junior high girl in camp rushes to the front, tears streaming down their faces, to rededicate their lives to the Lord. And then the junior high boys rush forward because there are crying junior high girls to hug. You know it's true.

Then there's the campfire—the perfect setting for relationships to experience their first spark (no pun intended). The sun has long ago set, and the sky is pitch-black except for the twinkling stars. There in the darkness, basking in the warm glow of the campfire, is the opportunity some have waited for all week—to hold hands with that special someone, the one they know they will spend the rest of their earthly lives with—at least until camp is over!

Around the campfire that Thursday evening is when my finest memory took place. The worship leader was allowing the kids to pick their favorite songs. We sang through the typical ones, "Kumbaya" and the like, and just when the night was about to conclude, a voice came from the back of the crowd, requesting one more song.

The voice was difficult to understand. It was Blake's. He wanted us to sing his favorite song, "Jesus Loves Me." The guitar began to strum, and there under the stars, the cicadas chirping in the background, we all sang in one voice the first verse and chorus, and then we stopped, because nobody knew the other verses of the song.

But Blake did. And so we all sat in silence as—in a voice no one could understand, but one that is music to God's ears—Blake sang the last verse of "Jesus Loves Me."

> Jesus loves me, he will stay
> Close beside me all the way;
> If I love him, when I die
> He will take me home on high.

Paul and Blake—both imprisoned—both sang.
Rebellious joy.

⌐ Reflection/Discussion ⌐

1. On your own, think about the difference between happiness and joy.

2. Do you find your joy to be dependent upon circumstances? If so, when do you most feel your joy being drained? Consider why.

3. Think about (and discuss) people you know who live with a sense of rebellious joy.

4. Joy is the result of the indwelling Holy Spirit. Consider ways you can remind yourself not to rely on your own effort in an attempt to sustain joy, but to rely on the person and the power of the Holy Spirit.

⌐ Prayer ⌐

Father, so many circumstances in life can easily steal our joy. By the power of your Holy Spirit, create in me a sense of joy that rebels against any and all difficult circumstances that come my way. May my joy be captivating to other people and also allow me the opportunity to talk about the source of my joy. In Jesus' name.

9

Risky

Several years ago in Korea, as the Communists were building a road, they discovered Pastor Kim and twenty-seven Christians he was leading, living in hand-dug tunnels beneath the earth.

The officials brought them out before a crowd of thirty thousand in the village of Gok San for a public trial and execution. "Deny Christ, or you will die," the Christians were told.

They refused.

At that point, the head officer ordered four children from the group seized and had them prepared for hanging. With ropes tied around their small necks, the officer again commanded the parents to deny Christ. Not one did. Instead, they told their children, "We will soon see you in heaven." The children quietly died.

The officer then called for a steamroller to be brought in. He forced the Christians to lie in its path. As its engine revved, they were given one last chance to recant their faith in Jesus. Again they refused.

As the steamroller inched forward, the Christians began to sing:

More love to Thee, O Christ, more love to Thee
Thee alone I seek, more love to Thee

Let sorrow do its work, more love to Thee
Then shall my latest breath whisper Thy praise
This be the parting cry my heart shall raise;
More love, O Christ, to Thee.[1]

I don't know the names of those who died that day, but I do know this, they were people who embraced risk.

Followers of Jesus always do.

When it comes to risk, there are two camps: those who embrace risk and those who don't. You don't usually "kind of" like taking risks. So which category do you fall in?

Risk takers . . .

- Bungee-jump. Those crazy people.

- Skydive. I will always wonder why people jump out of perfectly good planes.

- Become fire fighters, killer-whale trainers, and drivers ed teachers.

- Smoke cigarettes while pumping gas into their car.

If you are a person who avoids risk . . .

- You probably still have cans of corn and bottles of water that you bought in preparation for Y2K.

- You always turn off your cell phone while pumping gas because the sign says that talking on the phone could cause an explosion . . . and you pray for the person at the next pump who is smoking.

- You probably don't fly in planes; it seems much too risky. By the way, I read recently that every year more people are killed by donkeys than in plane crashes. Just sayin'.

1. Story adapted from *Jesus Freaks*, dc Talk (Minneapolis: Bethany House, 1999), 124–125.

So some people embrace risk while others don't, but the reality is that risk is a side effect that comes with living life.

It is unavoidable.

It is inevitable.

Most likely you began your day by waking up in a bed. Did you know that every year over five thousand people check into emergency rooms with pillow-related injuries? Sleeping is a risky venture.

After getting out of bed you probably used the bathroom. You should know that forty thousand Americans suffer a toilet-related injury of some kind. Whether you realize it or not, when you use the porcelain throne, the potty, or whatever you like to call it, you are living on the edge. (Actually, sitting on the edge.)

You drive? Most people do. You should know the U.S. Department of Transportation reports that someone is involved in a car accident every ten seconds.

So you thought you were a cautious person. But the truth is, you are an adrenaline junkie; you might as well start swallowing fire.

Larry Laudan, a philosopher of science, has spent years assessing risk management. In his book *Danger Ahead*, he summarizes his findings into nineteen principles, and principle number one is: *Everything is risky.*[2]

The same is true of living the Christian life. You cannot be a follower of Jesus—you cannot be a part of his church—without inheriting a certain level of risk. It has always been a bit risky to follow Christ. More than a bit, actually.

Recently I have been studying the passages where Jesus called his first disciples. Matthew, a tax collector, left his livelihood, his family, his financial security for the sake of following this poor Jewish teacher named Jesus; that is a risky proposition.

2. Larry Laudan, *Danger Ahead* (New York: Wiley, 1997).

Then Peter and John were called. They were fishermen by trade. It wasn't a glamorous living, for sure, but it was a living, and it was most likely the only trade they knew. Yet when Jesus invited them to follow him, we are told they left their nets behind. To us that may just sound like a Sunday school lesson, but for them it was a significant risk.

As you watch the events of the early church unfold, you could easily come to the conclusion that not only did believers accept risk, it seems they embraced it.

In Acts 14 we find Paul preaching in a city called Lystra. Apparently his message wasn't well received, because afterward he was beaten to the brink of death, dragged outside the city gates, and left to die. When he came to, he immediately went back into the city to preach again.

In Acts 7 a believer named Stephen was seized by the leaders because of his preaching, and false witnesses testified against him. "Are these charges true?" the high priest then asked. Now that was a defining moment. Stephen could have backpedaled a bit, apologized for the confusion, and carried on with his life. Instead, he began preaching another sermon about Jesus, and so out of anger they dragged him out of the city and stoned him to death.

Some people run away from risk, others seem to embrace it. Like Jesus- followers.

Yet Jesus' disciples didn't choose to be involved in risky scenarios simply for the thrill of it. Dodging stones wasn't exhilarating, and I have to believe they were not just a bunch of ragtag individuals with a martyr complex. Really, I think there is a pretty simple explanation for their behavior.

When I say risk, I mean faith.

Someone once said the best way to spell faith is R-I-S-K. Where there is no risk, there is no faith. Hebrews 11:1 says, "Faith is confidence in what we hope for and assurance about what we do not see." There is just a certain amount of risk involved with building your life on the existence of a God we cannot see, or touch, or feel. Even beyond that, it should come as no surprise that the church has always been wired with some risk. After all, we exist to serve a man who was such a threat to his culture that they murdered him on a cross. So the people of the first church did not embrace risk just for the sake of embracing it; instead, they were driven by their undying faith in Jesus. Where there is a strong faith, when there are crosses involved, there is certain to be some risk.

Perhaps that is why we tend to shy away from any type of risk. We are encouraged to have a plan B, money stashed away for rainy days, and a nice retirement waiting for us. We are trained to be creatures of comfort. We relax in La-Z-Boys and sleep at night in Select Comfort beds. Most of us will do whatever it takes to be comfortable.

Unfortunately, for some of us, our preoccupation with comfort has seeped into our faith. Some say, "I will go anywhere, give anything, say anything—as long as there is no risk, as long as I have some kind of guarantee that I won't get hurt, or rejected, or fired, or evicted."

This would be an easier discussion if only "other people" have been affected by the risk-avoidance mentality. I have been affected as well, and most likely you have too. So let me ask again, how do you handle risk? More specifically, how do you respond when your faith in Jesus compels you to take a risk? How do you react when the stakes are high? Or when you have something to lose?

Now, risk comes in many different packages, and at many different levels. It may be financial, emotional, relational, or physical. But whatever it looks like, how do you handle risk? Do you avoid it? Ignore it? Explain it away? Or do you embrace it as a necessary part of your faith in Christ?

My fear is that too many of us have adopted a faith that involves no risk. Our idea of following Jesus looks more like a safe walk in a park than a dangerous journey through mountainous terrain. The reality is, when you choose to follow Jesus, when you build your life on your faith in him, you are most likely going to be led to places you would rather not go. You might be compelled to give more than makes sense. You might be required to forsake dreams, cash out retirement portfolios, and leave family and friends behind. You might be called to live in a culture where you are the minority, a place where your language is not spoken and your faith is not tolerated. Jesus might nudge you to have a conversation you have always dreaded. Following him means a life of loving the unlovable, forgiving the unforgivable, and sometimes doing the undesirable.

I know how all of this sounds. A bit radical. A bit risky.

But following Jesus always has been. Ask Matthew, Peter, and John.

If we lived with the same blatant disregard for risk as the first church did, no insurance company in the world would write us a life insurance policy.

The Holy Spirit who empowered the believers in the first church happens to be the same Holy Spirit who lives in us. Sure, two thousand years have passed, but his desire, ability, and power hasn't changed.

But maybe we have changed. Perhaps we have chosen, or at least settled for, a safer faith.

I know that statement is not true about everyone. Maybe you are living in the midst of a dangerous, risky life of faith, but if you are, that makes you the exception to the rule.

In all of this talk about risky faith, you could easily draw the wrong conclusions or make rash decisions. Living a life of risky faith does not require you to pursue martyrdom, not at all. We tend to associate risk with literal life-and-death situations, but when it comes to our faith, that is not necessarily the case. For some it is, but not for most. For most of us, living with a risky faith does not mean standing in front of a firing squad, but rather that you are willing to cling to Jesus and his desires for your life even when there is something at stake, like . . .

Your job.

Your financial security.

Your reputation.

Your dreams.

And possibly, one day, your life.

We would all like to believe we would be ready to die if that is what our faith required, but honestly, if we are not willing to give up a job, or an extra vacation, or one layer of comfort for our faith, we most likely won't respond well when the steamroller starts inching forward.

⌐── Reflection/Discussion ──⌐

1. Would you categorize yourself as a risk-taker or a risk-avoider? Explain.

2. How does your approach toward risk affect your faith? Give specific examples.

3. Do you think it is possible to follow Jesus without inheriting certain risks? If you conclude risks are necessary, give examples of risks that must be assumed in following Jesus.

4. If you were willing to embrace risk as a part of your faith, how different would your life look? Be specific.

⌐ Prayer ⌐

Father, create in me a willingness to embrace risk for the sake of following you. Constantly remind me that my safety is not in my financial security, or reputation, or career, but in you and you alone. Lead me where you want me to go and to do what you want me to do, when it is comfortable and safe and when it is not. Lord, help me to evaluate my life honestly and see where I have stopped short of following you for the sake of safety, and then to make changes accordingly that I may follow you well. In Jesus' name.

10

Relentless

Theologian Frederick Buechner wrote, "Every age has produced fairy tales." Sounds poetic, yet it's true. Visit any people group, in any country, tribe, or village in the world, and you will find they have their own version of fairy tales. Evidence suggests we have been designed with a natural affinity for fairy tales. From a young age, little girls dream of becoming a queen or princess. You do not have to teach them that—the dream almost seems to be wired into their DNA. Similarly, little boys dream of becoming a valiant war hero or of bravely fighting a dragon. They might even entertain dreams of becoming a prince, because the prince always gets the princess.

There is something about fairy tales that never grows old. Children can be read the same story over and over again, and yet every time is like the first time. Even though they can recite many of the words from memory, there remains something captivating about having the fairy tale read to them. Nonetheless, at some point along the path of growing up, the tattered books get put up on the top shelf or maybe even packed away in the attic to collect dust, and reading fairy tales becomes a thing of the past.

We may have outgrown reading fairy tales, but we have not outgrown our attraction to fairy tales, especially their foundation: hope. Just listen to our language closely:

I hope I will meet Mr. (or Mrs.) Right one day.
I hope the economy begins to recover soon.
I hope I am able to live a long, healthy life.
I hope my child will choose a good mate.
I hope the medical tests come back positive (or negative).

You only need to add a few words to officially make these fairy tales—something like ". . . and they all lived happily ever after."

Almost every fairy tale is woven with a thread of hope. A good fairy tale pulls back the curtain on reality and suggests there is something more to life. A frog doesn't have to stay a frog forever; he can become a prince. Cinderella does not have to remain trapped in her oppressive life; she becomes a princess. If you read between the lines, fairy tales are laced with the possibility of transformation; they are filled with hope. Hope whispers of greater things to come. Life, as we know it, does not have to stay the same.

Look around you and it's easy to see that people are craving hope. No wonder. Life just has a way of knocking the breath out of our lungs and beating us down. You could probably deal with a frustrating relationship, or a difficult economy, or financial pressure, or a stressful job, but when you are being pounded by all of those simultaneously, it can be too much to bear, so slowly but surely the clouds roll in and darkness sets into your life.

There was a skillful artist who painted a bleak, winter landscape. A mountainside was covered with ice and snow, pine trees were straining against the cold wind, and icicles were hanging from the roof of a lonely cabin nestled against the side of a hill. It was a harsh, desolate scene. But then with just one touch of his brush, the artist transformed the picture completely. He dipped the tip of his brush in yellow and painted a golden glow in the cabin window. The painting took on an entirely different feel. That glow in the window communicated life, warmth, safety, hospitality, and hope.

A lot of people are stumbling through life, a glazed expression in their eyes, looking for a touch of yellow. The picture of their lives is bleak, lonely, or even icy; maybe the best description would be hopeless. A list of the greatest epidemics of our day would likely begin with AIDS and cancer, but maybe hopelessness should be added to the list.

One of the greatest tragedies in life is a hopeless person. They are not hard to recognize. They have no bounce in their step. No shine in their eye. And most of the time there is no smile on their face. Sadly, hopelessness is spreading like a contagious disease. Every year the suicide rate continues to climb. I want to be very sensitive with the issue of suicide, because I know many times there are some incredibly difficult circumstances involved and so I do not want to oversimplify the issue. However, at some level, suicide is the result of a deep and dominating sense of hopelessness. Now, maybe you haven't considered suicide, but possibly at some point you have become convinced that there is no hope. That is a lie authored and told by Satan. According to the Bible, every day Satan only has three things on his agenda: steal, kill, and destroy. Maybe it would be appropriate to put it like this: Satan's desire is to steal hope, to kill hope, and to destroy hope because he knows that hope is like oxygen for our souls. Hope is the difference between life and death.

But hope is not enough.

See, hope is only as powerful as the object or subject you are placing your hope in. And so the question must always be asked,

"What are you placing your hope in?" Maybe we shouldn't move any further without answering that question, not out loud—that could be awkward if you are sitting in a public place reading this—but silently answer that question right now to yourself. If the truth be told, if your soul were laid bare for everyone to see, what is your hope in?

For a lot of people, their hope is in . . .

Success. People might not say their hope is in success, but their lives say so. The evidence may be the endless hours you spend at work; you are always the last one to leave and the first one to show up. Even when you are away from the office you may constantly find your mind wandering back to the work you have waiting for you. Maybe your time commitment seems like you are trying to be diligent about your career, but there is a fine line between being diligent at your job and your job becoming your identity and your source of hope.

Wealth. Someone, not so wise, once said, "Money makes the world go round." I suppose that phrase means money is required to live, and that is true. Life isn't free. At some level money is a necessity of life; some would say money is an evil necessity of life. However, for a lot of people, money is much more than a necessity. It is an infatuation, or an obsession. If you don't think so, find an episode of *Fear Factor* and watch people eat roaches, swim with alligators, and submerge their heads in an aquarium full of snakes all for a few dollars. Some people will do anything for money. The commonly accepted perspective toward money is the more, the better. Now, money in and of itself is not evil. People often misquote the Bible and say, "Money is the root of all evil." It actually says, "The love of money is a root of all kinds of evil" (1 Timothy 6:10). The reason people fall in love with money is that subconsciously they become convinced that money is a source of salvation—that with enough money they can be saved from discomfort, boredom, and dissatisfaction.

When money seems like a source of salvation, they place all of their hope in their money.

Vanity. Our physical bodies were designed to be the shell for our souls, but now, especially in our culture, our bodies are treated as idols. Not only do we treat other people's bodies as an object of worship, many of us treat our own in much the same way. When we see ourselves in a mirror, we don't bow down as people would with an idol, but many of us are consumed with what we see in the mirror. Either we're consumed with frustration because we do not have the appearance we long to have, or with pride because we like what we see. Either way it is easy to begin to treat vanity itself as our source of hope. Our culture has trained us to think this way because you can achieve a lot of fame and fortune with the right face, or with chiseled abs, or a head full of beautiful hair. So subconsciously, people are trained to treat their own physical bodies as their golden ticket, or as their source of hope.

No matter how innocent it may seem, if your hope is in success, or wealth, or vanity, you are only setting yourself up for disappointment. Success, wealth, and vanity all have one thing in common: all make promises they cannot keep.

Success may offer you opportunity and provision and praise for a while, but the day will come when someone else will sit in your chair, your nameplate will be taken down from the door, and your parking spot will be given away. They may hang your picture on a wall, but the sobering reality is at some point no one will even remember your name. As an example, most Americans cannot name more than a few presidents, and one cannot achieve more worldly success than serving as president of the United States! So success may promise greater things to come, but it is a promise it cannot keep.

Wealth promises safety, security, and satisfaction, and may be able to do so for a while, but not for long. Houses burn down, stock markets crash, and eventually the line goes flat on the heart monitor, and no amount of money can buy the next breath. You have probably heard the phrase, "You can't take it with you when you die." It's true. Your funeral procession may include many great cars, but there is not going to be a U-Haul truck. Wealth may promise greater things to come, but that is a promise it cannot keep.

Vanity may be the biggest fraud when it comes to offering hope of something greater. Physiologists say that the human body reaches its peak somewhere in the mid-twenties, and from there our body begins the slow process of dying. As the months and years pass, looking in the mirror is enough to remind us that vanity, beauty, and strength will only last a little while. Wrinkles sneak in around our eyes, deep lines begin to carve our faces, gray hair begins to overtake our heads, or maybe you have been overtaken by invisible hair, otherwise known as baldness. Joints begin to tighten, muscles start to ache, and eyesight diminishes. If your physical body is your source of hope, it is not difficult to conclude that you are going to face inevitable disappointment. Slim-Fast, Rogaine, Mary Kay, and Botox will fight the battle for a while, but eventually gravity and nature will have their way. Vanity can promise the hope of something greater, but that is a promise it cannot keep.

The only thing more heartbreaking than someone with no hope is a person who clings to a false hope. As Christians we don't have to settle for a temporary hope, or a shallow hope, or a false hope. We have an eternal hope—a hope that promises that something greater is to come. That is what makes Christianity distinct from every other religious system in the world. We do not have to put our hope in a belief system, or a list of rules, or in our own feeble attempts at morality. Our hope is not in a thing, our hope is a person; his name is Jesus. In the Christian life hope is not an afterthought, nor is hope a pipe dream.

When you read through the Bible, you find traces of hope on almost every page. In the New Testament the apostle Paul wrote thirteen letters, most of them to specific churches, and as you read his writings he is constantly pointing his readers to the hope we have in Christ. One refrain in Paul's writings could be summarized this way: "Do not forget the great hope we have in Christ."

Whether you are in good times or bad . . . don't forget the hope we have in Christ.

Whether in wealth or poverty . . . don't forget the hope we have in Christ.

Whether in sickness or in health . . . don't forget the hope we have in Christ.

When you are in the midst of tragedy or triumph . . . don't forget the hope we have in Christ.

The writer of Hebrews describes our hope this way: "We have this hope as an anchor for the soul" (6:19).

Maybe that is the best picture to associate with the hope we have in Christ. No matter how turbulent the waters of life get, no matter how hard the wind of disappointment blows, we can remain stable and steadfast because we have this anchor attached to our souls called hope. Hope is the gentle voice in the depth of our souls that whispers greater things to come—maybe not in this life, but in the life to come.

Our hope in Christ should change the way we face life.

One of the most captivating passages in the New Testament is in the book of 2 Corinthians:

Therefore we do not lose heart. Though outwardly we are wasting away, yet inwardly we are being renewed day by day. For our light and momentary troubles are achieving for us an eternal glory that far outweighs them all. So we fix our eyes not on what is seen, but on what is unseen, since what is seen is temporary, but what is unseen is eternal.

2 Corinthians 4:16–18

Here is the captivating phrase: "our light and momentary troubles." If you don't know much about Paul's life, you might skim over those words without thinking twice, but when you understand the intense level of suffering and persecution he experienced on a daily basis, it almost seems irrational to describe his troubles as "light and momentary."

I have worked much harder, been in prison more frequently, been flogged severely, and been exposed to death again and again. Five times I received from the Jews the forty lashes minus one. [They were only allowed to give thirty-nine lashes because that was considered to be the brink of death.] Three times I was beaten with rods, once I was pelted with stones, three times I was shipwrecked, I spent a night and a day in the open sea, I have been constantly on the move. I have been in danger from rivers, in danger from bandits, in danger from my fellow Jews, in danger from Gentiles; in danger in the city, in danger in the country, in danger at sea; and in danger from false believers. I have labored and toiled and have often gone without sleep; I have known hunger and thirst and have often gone without food; I have been cold and naked. Besides everything else, I face daily the pressure of my concern for all the churches.

2 Corinthians 11:23–28

Those are light and momentary troubles? The only reason Paul could confidently and seriously write those words is because he knew the hope we have in Christ. When you know that hope, the way you face life is changed. Still, there are no guarantees all troubles will fade away, or that turmoil will disappear, or that you will become immune to struggles. Jesus said, "In this world you will have trouble" (John 16:33). Health challenges will still occur; bankruptcies will continue to become more common; relationships will crumble around you.

Yet in the midst of it all, if you are following Jesus, you will feel the anchor in your soul take hold and will hear the still, small whisper remind you that greater things are to come.

When your hope is in Christ, even on the darkest days of life when your stomach is in knots, the lump is in your throat, and the sky seems like it is falling, you can join Paul in saying, "[I will] not lose heart . . . for our light and momentary troubles are achieving for us an eternal glory. . . ."

Our hope in Christ should change the way we face life. But that is not all.

Our hope in Christ should also change the way we face death.

When researchers ask people to name their greatest fear, death is always near the top of the list (strangely enough, usually right under the fear of public speaking, which explains why at a funeral most people would rather be the person in the casket than the one speaking the eulogy). I understand why so many people fear death—the timing of death is so uncertain and is often accompanied by pain and suffering. But maybe the reason people fear death is that it seems so final. To avoid the final curtain, many spend hours a day working out, take handfuls of vitamins or other supplements, get shots, have surgeries, try to eat right and sleep well, and get things nipped, tucked, and "lipo-sucked," all in the name of living healthy lives. People would say they are just trying to improve the quality of their lives, but there is a deeper motivation: to increase the *quantity* of their lives. But here is the reality you already know: Everyone dies—ten out of ten people. So the question is not "Will you die?" or "Will the people you love die?" The real question is, "How will you face death?" Will you try your best to avoid it? Will you fear it? Or will you cling tighter than ever to your hope in Christ?

A Christian missionary named Graham Staines moved from Australia to India in 1965 to provide care for the poor and helpless in the name of Jesus. He met and married his wife, Gladys, and together they continued in their good work. As the years passed their family grew. First they had a daughter, and later had two sons, Timothy and Philip. They were a happy family who had committed their lives to serving Jesus. In early 1999, however, dark clouds of tragedy rolled into their lives, and it seemed like all "yellow" had been erased. Graham had taken his sons, ten and six years old, with him on an evangelistic crusade. After a long day they settled into their old station wagon for the night. After they drifted into sleep, a politically charged mob of over a hundred men blocked the doors of their station wagon. After breaking the windows they poured gasoline on and in the vehicle, lit a match, and then stood shouting political slogans as the father and his two sons burned alive.

The community was stunned, and on the day of the funeral, more than a thousand mourners packed into the small building in support of Gladys and her daughter. The funeral was televised nationally and covered by every major media outlet in India. With the cameras rolling, Gladys stepped up to the microphone, and in a shaky but compassionate voice said, "I forgive the men who did this to my family." And then with her daughter they sang, "Because He Lives," beautifully declaring that because Christ lives, all their fear was gone and they could face tomorrow.

The hope we can have in Christ is not a naïve hope. There is reason—good reason—behind it. Tens of millions have gone down to the grave, but only one has come back.

Alive.

On a Friday afternoon Jesus was nailed to a cross, but on Sunday morning he turned death's door into a revolving door.

Because he lives not only can we endure the darkest days of life, but we can also mockingly stare death in the face. The Bible says that because Jesus conquered death we too will conquer death. That is our hope. That is the whisper of greater things to come.

I couldn't rightfully end a chapter on hope without telling you about my dear friend and my second most favorite woman. By the way, my wife knows about her and is fine with my talking about her this way. Her name is Hildegarde. She is eighty-seven years young.

About eighteen months ago, just after I moved to northern Kentucky, I met Hildegarde. Due to some health reasons, she had been unable to attend church on Sunday for several weeks. A friend of hers emailed me and asked if I would visit Hildegard at home because she was eager to meet the new minister personally.

At that first visit, Hildegarde had me at hello. We talked a blue streak for an hour or so, and when I left, I promised her I would be back. And I have gone back once a week, sometimes twice, for the last year and a half. Spending time with Hildegarde has never been a burden, but a blessing.

She has a smile that lights up any room and a contagious laugh. She is a beautiful woman, but time has had its way with her. Her eyes still shine, but her eyesight is now blurry. Her hair has gracefully faded from black to shining silver. When I met her, I noticed the lines on her face, but as I have grown to know her I have learned those lines tell her story—a story that includes joy and laughter and love. Still, if her life story were written in the form of a book, the longest chapter would be called "Heartache."

It was on a Saturday afternoon almost seventy years ago that Hildegarde and Alvin looked into each other's eyes and promised to love each other until death separated them. For some, wedding vows are a matter of routine. For Alvin and Hildegarde, those words were a promise they refused to break.

For sixty-three years they lived as husband and wife, in good times and in bad, in sickness and in health, in poverty and in wealth, until death came uninvited.

Hildegarde was left alone to bury her husband, but it wasn't the first funeral she had planned in her lifetime. Hildegarde is mother to two boys. Donald was born December 11, 1946, and Timothy was born November 5, 1951. Like all brothers they laughed and played and fought. Sometimes they were the best of friends, other days they were each other's greatest enemies; but at the end of every day they were brothers and they were loved dearly. Hildegarde cherished the privilege of raising two boys. She was a schoolteacher, but she took an extended leave to focus on being a mommy until the boys were old enough to go off to school. Before Alvin and Hildegarde had a chance to blink their boys had grown into men.

After high school, Tim attended the University of Cincinnati. Like all college students, his life was filled with deadlines and homework and pressure. So many questions swirled through his mind. What would he major in? What career would he have? Would there be a special someone? But just before his twentieth birthday, before he could even fully answer those seemingly life-and-death questions, he was in a car wreck. For Tim there was no more life, just death.

Then Don.

As Don grew into a man, he set aside his childhood dreams when he willingly enlisted in the United States Army and was sent to fight in the Vietnam conflict. Don trained as a pilot, so after he returned to civilian life that became the most natural career option for him. The cockpit became his office, his comfort zone, and sadly, his grave.

On June 23, 1972, just seven months after his brother's death, Don was instructed to take off in a plane that had landed short of the runway and to land it properly and safely. That was his intention, but it never happened. Shortly after getting the plane off the ground, the plane returned to the ground. You know how the story ended.

Another pile of wrecked steel. Another funeral to plan.

One year. Two sons.

Dead.

Needless to say, Hildegarde has been slammed with one agony after another; the waves have been relentless.

So is her hope.

Whether holding her baby boys in her arms, or standing next to one freshly dug grave, and then another, and then another, she has had a whisper in her heart shouting there is something greater coming. That whisper is the anchor of her soul. That whisper is her hope.

Jesus rose to live again.

So will her boys. And so will she.

Al, Hildegarde, Don, and Tim will live happily ever after. With Jesus. Together. Forever.

It sounds like a fairy tale, but it is the gospel truth.

⌐ Reflection/Discussion ⌐

1. As you honestly evaluate your life, in whom or what have you placed your hope? If you ask people close to you to answer this question about you, how do you think they would answer?

2. When you find yourself daydreaming about life, what do you daydream about? Perhaps this is an indication you are placing hope in something temporary. Spend some time evaluating your daydreams and consider what they might say about where your hope is found.

3. The author of Hebrews talks about the hope we have as Christians as being "an anchor for the soul" (6:19). In the midst of difficult circumstances, do you sense your hope holding strong? Or do you feel like you are beginning to drift?

4. Does your hope in Christ change the way you face life and death? Explain.

┌── Prayer ──┘

Father, thank you for the hope we have in you. Because of Jesus' death and resurrection from the dead, even death—our greatest fear—is nothing to be feared. When the difficult moments of life come and suffering shows up unexpected and uninvited, remind us of the great hope we have in you and because of you. May we have a hope that is relentless. May our hope radically change the way we face life and death. In Jesus' name.

11

Scandalous

Philip Yancey in his book *What's So Amazing About Grace?* relates a story from a friend who worked with the down-and-out in Chicago:

> A prostitute came to me in wretched straits, homeless, sick, unable to buy food for her two-year-old daughter. Through sobs and tears she told me that she had been renting out her daughter—two years old!—to men. . . . She made more renting out her daughter for an hour than she could earn on her own in a night. She had to do it, she said, to support her own drug habit. I could hardly bear to hear her sordid story. For one thing it made me legally liable—I'm required to report cases of child abuse. I had no idea what to say to this woman.
>
> At last I asked if she had ever thought of going to a church for help. I will never forget the look of pure, naïve shock that crossed her face. "Church!" she cried. "Why would I ever go there? I was already feeling terrible about myself. They'd just make me feel worse."[1]

1. Philip Yancey, *What's So Amazing About Grace?* (Grand Rapids, MI: Zondervan, 1997), 11.

When I read that story I find myself asking, Why is it that some of the same people who once ran hard and fast toward Jesus in the Gospels are now running equally hard and fast away from Jesus' church? We can attempt to explain the difficult reality away, or rationalize the trend, or simply ignore the pattern, but the truth remains that the people who once were so incredibly attracted to Jesus are now in many cases repulsed by Jesus' bride, the church.

In the Gospels, Jesus was at least one time accused of being a friend of sinners (Mark 2:13–17). And Jesus himself would say he was guilty as charged. Where you found Jesus, you were also sure to find the cast outs, the down and outers, the overlooked, the undervalued. He had meals inside the home of a tax collector, his ministry was in part financially supported by at least one prostitute, and several members of his inner circle were fishermen—not known to be the most prim and proper men around. There was one woman who had been married five times already and was living with a sixth man. Then there was the man who died on a cross next to Jesus who was also strangely drawn to him. So many of the people Jesus associated with weren't going to be found on any Who's Who lists. In fact, some were more likely to be found on the most wanted list, yet these people were almost magnetically attracted to Jesus.

If I were to explain that attraction in one word, it would be *grace*. The biblical word *grace* is translated from the Greek word *charis*, which means an unmerited favor or gift. So grace is getting what you do not deserve and could not possibly earn. This is a working definition, but grace cannot really be explained, it has to be experienced.

In Bible times, the people who chased after Jesus believed if they could get to him and experience his grace, their lives could be forever changed. Many people today seem to have adopted the opposite mind-set; get your life changed and then come to Jesus. I wouldn't say we cognitively believe that to be true, but somewhere that message has been communicated because it is so widely believed. No doubt every one of us have encountered a person who has said things like, "I've been meaning to come to church, but I'm just trying to get a grip on this drinking thing first," or "I'd like to have Jesus involved in my life, but I have a lot of cleaning up to do first." Perhaps you have had similar thoughts. Though that mind-set is adopted with the best of intentions, it's like saying, "As soon as I get well, I'll go to the hospital."

The seeming lack of grace exhibited by some professing Christians doesn't help. Perhaps you have seen the T-shirts or bumper stickers that say, "I love Jesus, I just don't like his followers." Someone once said, "The greatest hindrance to the spread of Christianity is Christians." I don't think those statements are totally valid, and at times they may be nothing more than an excuse, but there is some level of truth there.

Tragic is the best word to describe this perception of some Christians because you cannot overemphasize the significance of grace to this movement called Christianity. Does grace need to be balanced with the importance of obedience? Yes, but that does not diminish the significance of grace. In fact, I would even be willing to take it this far: Where there is no grace, there is no Christianity. The Bible does not say that, but the implication is everywhere.

I set out to trace *grace* throughout the Gospels and was stunned to find out the word is used only once:

> For the law was given through Moses; grace and truth came through Jesus Christ.
>
> John 1:17

Because the word is so rare, you could easily conclude that grace didn't play a dominant role in the early church, but look more deeply at what John 1:17 says. In essence, Jesus Christ was grace personified. More specifically, he ushered grace into a graceless world. Even if you weren't aware of that piece of Scripture and you simply studied Jesus' life and ministry, it wouldn't take long to reach the same conclusion. If a first-century CSI (Crime Scene Investigation) crew followed Jesus around, they would have found the same thing at every scene: the evidence of grace. If the investigators interviewed eyewitnesses to the work and movements of Jesus, I'll bet they would hear phrases like *captivating* or *breathtaking*, or maybe even a word like *perplexing*. People back then just weren't accustomed to the whole concept of grace. I told you that Jesus ushered grace into a graceless world, and that is a pretty accurate description of the first-century world. It was an eye-for-an-eye, tooth-for-a-tooth society, where you get what you deserve, nothing more and nothing less. You lived by the law and died by the law, and so when this man named Jesus came along, whose work and ministry was defined by grace, it would have gone against the grain of society.

An eyewitness to an account that is recorded in Luke 7 would likely use the word *scandalous* to describe Jesus' behavior. It started when Jesus was invited into the home of a Pharisee to share a meal. That detail alone is worth noting. Jesus and the Pharisees mixed almost as well as oil and water, and in the first century, sharing a meal together was quite an intimate arrangement.

We pick up the story with Jesus reclining at the table:

> A woman in that town who lived a sinful life learned that Jesus was eating at the Pharisee's house, so she came there with an alabaster jar of perfume. As she stood behind him at his feet weeping, she began to wet his feet with her tears. Then she wiped them with her hair, kissed them and poured perfume on them.
>
> Luke 7:37–38

Now I have to hit pause on the story right there for a moment. These verses are saturated with implications. The scenery and the characters involved seem like they belong in a spiritual soap opera. We have a Pharisee, who would have been happy to tell you that he had spirituality all figured out; he knew what prayers to pray and when to pray them, he gave his money at the temple, he likely had a majority of the Old Testament Scriptures memorized, he was undoubtedly a proud owner of a prayer shawl with extra-long tassels that served as a spiritual résumé of sorts. If this man was one thing, he was religious.

Then there was Jesus.

At the time, he was quickly gaining popularity with the common people in society, all the while growing increasingly unpopular with the religious authorities. There were whispers he had not so subtly been claiming to be God, so some had concluded he had gone crazy and was just another revolutionary who would soon fade away. Others were adamant he really was divine. Either way, this Jesus was at the center of many conversations.

Then there was a woman.

We know almost nothing about her except that she had lived a sinful life. The evidence would suggest she was a prostitute. That would explain why she had a reputation all over town and why her hair had been let down instead of hidden under a veil.

So how does a woman of her standing get into Simon's house in the first place? Good question, and there is a good answer. During feasts like this one, people were often allowed to observe the festivities, sometimes talk with the guests, and even receive some of the leftovers. Most likely this woman was simply taking advantage of that custom in order to be near Jesus. But she wasn't content with just that. She began anointing his feet and wiping perfume on them with her hair. At that point, undoubtedly, the room fell silent and all eyes locked on Jesus to see how he would respond.

When the Pharisee who had invited him saw this, he said to himself, "If this man were a prophet, he would know who is touching him and what kind of a woman she is— that she is a sinner." Jesus answered him, "Simon, I have something to tell you."

Luke 7:39–40

Simon is oblivious to the fact that Jesus has already read his mind: He knows the condescending, judgmental thoughts Simon is entertaining. When Simon says, "Tell me, teacher," Jesus continues:

"Two people owed money to a certain moneylender. One owed him five hundred denarii, and the other fifty. Neither of them had the money to pay him back, so he forgave the debts of both. Now which of them will love him more?"
Simon replied, "I suppose the one who had the bigger debt forgiven."
"You have judged correctly," Jesus said.

vv. 41–43

Simon answered the question correctly, but there is no way of knowing if he fully understood Jesus' teaching. Much more important is if *we* grasp the principle being taught. Simon and the apparent prostitute were both equally unable to pay their debt. They were both totally dependent on his grace. Jesus had not stooped any lower by letting the woman touch him than he had by agreeing to share a meal with Simon.

Not so sure that Simon would have seen it that way. Actually, I'm sure he didn't. Do you?

Earlier I mentioned that people may tend to be turned off by the church because of an apparent lack of grace, but I'm not sure that is the real issue at hand. I do not believe our biggest problem, as a church, is a lack of grace but a common misunderstanding of grace. This misunderstanding is a symptom of what I call the Simon complex.

The Simon complex causes us to believe that Jesus' grace is more than enough to cleanse us, and save us, and change us, but it might not be enough for certain other people. So we begin to create boundaries for God's grace. We may know better, but one way we subtly do this is by ranking sins. Some sins, like gossip, we are not prone to take very seriously at all. We can brush that under the rug or look the other way. However, other sins, like murder or sexual immorality of some kind, or rape, are in another category altogether.

Now understand, this isn't something we tangibly or even intentionally do, but the behavior exposes itself in the way we tend to love people or not, or forgive people or not. Not necessarily with words, but with actions we draw lines in the sand—we create boundaries for God's grace. The lines are always drawn far enough out so that we are included in the grace, but that is where the line usually stops, leaving groups of people, or "types" of sinners, standing outside the parameters of God's grace.

This is the Simon complex. Read again Simon's reaction:

When the Pharisee [Simon] who had invited him saw this, he said to himself, "If this man were a prophet, he would know who is touching him and what kind of a woman she is—that she is a sinner."

Luke 7:39

Simon had created boundaries.

The woman was on the outside, looking in.

She was just too sinful.

Her sins were of the major variety—a 10 on the "sin scale."

Simon had drawn lines.

Let me get back to my original question: Why are the same people who once ran hard and fast toward Jesus now running equally hard and fast away from the church?

I am not a doctor, but the church as a whole seems to be

suffering from the Simon complex; we have set too many boundaries. As a result the world no longer recognizes us as the oasis of grace that the church was intended to be.

Theologian Gordon MacDonald has said, "The world can do almost anything as well or better than the church. You need not be a Christian to build houses, feed the hungry, or heal the sick. There is only one thing the world cannot do. It cannot offer grace."

If there is just one thing that should make us distinct as a church from the world around us, it should be that grace can be found in our midst. For that to be true we have to both acknowledge and battle the Simon complex—the idea that we are within the bounds of God's grace, but some others aren't.

Simon drew lines. So have I. Have you?

I think there are two treatments for this Simon complex. First, **we need to be always reminded of our condition.**

Over the years, I have encountered many people both inside and outside of the church who were actively involved in AA. One friend of mine was going to be celebrating his thirtieth year of sobriety, so he invited me to his AA meeting. I was captivated by what took place. The sense of community was impressive, and I was encouraged to see the level of accountability that was required. But one thing really stood out. Many of you already know this, but whenever someone speaks to the rest of the group, they identify themselves according to this pattern: "Hi, my name is Jamie, and I am an alcoholic." I have been told this reminds them that alcoholism is a disease that requires an ongoing battle. But also, by identifying themselves in that way, the playing field always stays level.

Perhaps that is what the church—and by the church, I mean *we*—needs more of: a willingness to constantly identify ourselves as who we really are and to be honest about our condition. I know I am being a bit idealistic, but wouldn't we experience a breath of fresh air if the church were a place where people were so transparent that they willingly identified themselves this way: "Hi, my name is Jamie. I struggle with sin daily, but I have been saved by grace"?

Again, by they, I mean *we*.

That statement of identification isn't just idealistic; it is actually quite theologically accurate.

> As for you, you were dead in your transgressions and sins, in which you used to live when you followed the ways of this world and of the ruler of the kingdom of the air, the spirit who is now at work in those who are disobedient. All of us also lived among them at one time, gratifying the cravings of our flesh and following its desires and thoughts. Like the rest, we were by nature deserving of wrath. But because of his great love for us, God, who is rich in mercy, made us alive with Christ even when we were dead in transgressions—it is by grace you have been saved.
>
> Ephesians 2:1–5

Paul wrote this letter to the Ephesians, and I have a hunch that if you met him personally, he might introduce himself this way: "Hi, I'm Paul. I struggle with sin, but I have been saved by grace." In another one of his letters, Paul even called himself the chief sinner, and I think Paul would tell you, "If God's grace can save me, God's grace can save anyone."

There is just something about being honest about our own condition and acknowledging our own dependence on grace that levels the playing field and causes the boundaries of God's grace to be stretched in our minds.

This leads me to the second treatment for the Simon complex. **We have to be willing to intentionally stretch the boundaries of God's grace in practical ways.**

Simply believing that God's grace can reach anyone is not enough. As the church we have been called to be the vessels of his grace. Understand, the boundaries for his grace will never be stretched unless we are willing to do the stretching.

So let me cut to the chase. I have been asking the questions; now let me make a statement.

We all have lines drawn.

It is likely you haven't noticed that you have drawn them, but if you looked hard enough, and you were honest enough, you would find them. So would I.

The real question is not whether or not we have drawn lines around God's grace, but where have they been drawn? Who are we keeping out?

For Simon, it was difficult for him to believe that God's grace could cover a woman who most likely was living a life of prostitution. She stood on the other side of the line.

Who stands on the other side of the line for you?

Is it a demographic group, a certain type of people? Is it individuals who live a different lifestyle from what you deem appropriate? Who is it? Let me get more specific. Perhaps it is the homosexual community, and you are just so appalled by their lifestyle that you cannot imagine God's grace extending that far. Maybe in your mind the line is drawn to exclude illegal immigrants. For some of you, it may be as simple as excluding people who are in the opposite political party from you. For others, you have set a boundary that keeps out people of other races. So who is it? Where have the lines been drawn?

Several years ago, I was preparing to share these same thoughts in a sermon. I was forced to look at myself in the mirror and wrestle with these same questions. The bad part about being a preacher is that you have to practice what you preach, or at least you should try. I honestly did some self-reflection and tried to determine who it was that I had excluded from God's grace.

People who hurt children.

People who badly hurt children.

People who kill children.

I still remember the day that I pulled into the parking lot of Dr. S's clinic.

Dr. S was an Iranian doctor.

An Iranian Muslim doctor.

An Iranian Muslim abortion doctor.

In some cases the word *doctor* is used very loosely.

His office building was a shabby, rickety old thing, the sort of shady place you would expect an abortion clinic to be. The mailbox was hanging from just one screw, and the door creaked a bit as it opened. Inside the lobby, the lights were dim much like the vibe I felt as I walked through the door. I went there with gifts in hand, with the simple intention of trying to get an opportunity to speak with the doctor for a few minutes. I simply wanted to let him know that though I passionately disagreed with his profession, there is a God and Savior who passionately loves him. Going to his office with such plans may sound heroic, but doing so was easy because I didn't anticipate they would let me speak to him. In fact, I hadn't even really thought through what I would say if given the opportunity. I calmly explained to the receptionist the purpose of my visit. She looked at me with a confused expression, and then she closed the window separating the office from the lobby. As I sat and waited, I remember having the distinct sensation that I was sitting in a graveyard.

I fully anticipated the receptionist returning to tell me the doctor was unwilling to speak with me, and so I was stunned when she opened the door and beckoned me back to his office. I sat down in the empty office, my heart pounding out of my chest, asking myself, *What am I doing here? And what am I going to say?* He finally came bounding through the office door, rattling the diplomas and pictures on the wall. He sat down at his desk and matter-of-factly asked why I had come. With my voice shaking, I explained that I simply came to apologize for the way Christians had treated him in the past. He just kept staring at me, waiting to hear why I really had come, and after a few moments of silence, he asked me again, "So why did you really come?" I said, "Sir, bottom line, I came to let you know that I love you and that Jesus loves you." The perplexed look on his face gradually became a look of pain. Through tears, he told me stories of young mothers who had come into his clinic and how he honestly believed he was trying to help them by destroying the life growing inside of them. What he didn't know is that as a pastor I have had women who have had abortions sit in my office and explain through tears how they feel like life had literally been sucked out of them. These are the cruel games Satan plays. At one point he compared aborting a child to a dentist removing a sore tooth. Interestingly, he seemed to so badly want my approval, which of course I could not give. However, I had not gone to his office to lash out at him but to show love. About an hour into our conversation, the nurse, who also happened to be his ex-wife, burst through the door and explained he had patients waiting and that I needed to leave, all the while staring me down. As she left, I said, "I see who wore the pants in that relationship." Just kidding. But I wanted to.

As the doctor stood, I said, "I have to share with you one more thing. As Christians, I'm sure you know what we are against because we are very quick to let people know. But do you know what we are for?"

He looked a bit confused and shook his head no. I said, "As followers of Jesus, we are about love, peace, patience, kindness, gentleness, and self-control." Then before leaving, I prayed with him and invited him to our church. The next week I walked out onto the platform to begin my message and felt a lump form in my throat when I looked out and saw Dr. S sitting in the front row. After the service, we sat in my office and talked about the Bible and Jesus. For several weeks he returned to listen to the teaching, and every week we would spend time in my office in discussion together.

I would love to tell you the story ended with Dr. S falling in love with Jesus, but as far as I know that hasn't happened. I do know that in that single instance I tried to stretch the boundaries of God's grace.

Another thing happened too. I started recovering from the Simon Complex. Slowly.

Whom do you need to visit? Where do you need to go?

An office? A house? An area of town?

Honestly answer this question. Then go. Don't stop and ask questions and chance getting lost in the what-ifs. Just go.

Walk.

Fly.

Drive.

Run.

But go.

Fast.

Before it's too late.

When Jesus began this movement called church, he dreamed his followers would live in such a way that when people of this world are hurting and broken, when they are defeated and empty, when they have gotten to the end of their rope, when people are needing a second chance, a fresh start, a clean slate, that they would come running with arms open wide to the church.

Not to a place, to a people.

And not just on Sunday.

Hopefully they will come running, and when they do, hopefully they will see us running too—not away, but toward them . . .

With arms open wide.

When arms are open wide, grace happens. Scandalous grace.

Ask Jesus. He knows.

He has the scars to prove it.

⌐ Reflection/Discussion ⌐

1. How has the Simon Complex affected your life? Where have you drawn lines? Whom have you kept out?

2. Talk about ways you can intentionally stretch the boundaries of God's grace in your circle of influence.

3. Identify possible reasons people may feel as if they have been rejected by the church. How can we change the perception?

4. Perhaps you are someone who was hesitant to become a part of the Christian faith because of a negative experience in your life with a church or another Christian. Talk about the experience and how it impacted your perception of the church. How can you use this experience to shape your own faith?

⌐ Prayer ⌐

Father, thank you for the grace you have poured into our lives. As the Bible says, it is by grace and grace alone that we have been saved. Teach us freely to share grace with others, the way we freely accept grace. Give us eyes to recognize where we have drawn lines that have excluded certain people or types of people from our circles of influence. Use us to stretch the boundaries of your grace in our neighborhoods and communities. And may we never pretend to be deserving of the grace we have been given by you. In Jesus' name.

12

Mad

Love.

No other word in the English language has been used and abused more. Not just by other people, but by me.

These are the things that I have said I loved over the last few weeks or so:

Chocolate shakes
Pepperoni pizza
P. F. Chang's
The NFL
My wife (these are in no particular order)
My two sons: Cy and Cruz
The new socks I was given for Christmas

Yes, that is how I have used the word *love* lately. But before you wag your finger at me, make your own list.

See, it's not just me.

Something has obviously gone wrong when we use the same

word to describe our feelings about greasy, fattening foods and our spouses. How romantic. Love.

I have no authority over the English language—not sure who does, but it seems like we need to create a new word for love, because now *love* means the same thing as *like*.

Before we were married, my wife actually did invent a new word. She more than liked me but wasn't ready to say she loved me (even though she did), so instead, one time she said, "I lyve you." *Ahhh*. That moment brought to you by Hallmark. Maybe we should all just start using that word when we really, really, really like something but *love* would be too strong a word.

Let me go first. I lyve pizza. I don't think it will catch on.

Love has been twisted, tainted, diluted. The word, at least. The truth is, even in its purest form, the word *love* falls short of capturing the idea. Trying to reduce the awe and wonder of love down to a single expression is like trying to capture the Atlantic Ocean in a toy bucket. When it comes to communicating the power and essence of love, you need more than a word. You need words. Lots of them to even get close.

Start tracing God's love through the Bible, and you will find his love is deeper than the deepest ocean and higher than the highest peak. His love is wider than the east is from the west. You would find that God's love for people is intense and relentless and endless. You would conclude that God's love is extravagant and unconditional and irresponsible.

From the very beginning of creation, God has gone to all lengths to show people how much he loves them. When it comes to love, you have to show and tell. And God did.

There is a story in the Old Testament where God is desperate to communicate his love to the people, but he knows it will take more than words. So he tells his prophet Hosea to do a pretty strange thing—to go to the bad part of town and find a prostitute named Gomer and marry her. Well, that's a lot to ask of a guy. I mean, it's one thing to marry a prostitute, but to marry a prostitute named Gomer? But Hosea does it. He goes into the red-light district of town, finds this prostitute named Gomer, and marries her. After a while, he's not just obeying God, he really does fall in love with her. He moves from going through the motions to being overcome with emotion.

Raw.

Real.

Unexpected.

Emotion.

Somehow, this whole thing is working. Their relationship transitions from being an arranged marriage to being a functioning, healthy marriage. But not for long. One day Hosea comes home, and the house is empty. The kids are there by themselves, and he gets a sick feeling in his stomach. He has a hunch. No, he *knows*. He runs as fast as he can to the red-light district, and there he sees his wife in the arms of another man, leading him into a cheap motel. Hosea cries out to God, "God, you told me to do this; I did it! You told me to marry her; I married her. And then this happens. What am I supposed to do now?"

God says, "Here is what you do. You go back and you find her again, and you buy her back again. You bring her home again, and you show your love to her again."

Hosea asks, "Why?" (Wouldn't you?)

And God answers, "So the people will know—they will understand just how much I love them."

That's love. Mad love.

Before I go any further with the story of Hosea, let me say this. When we study the Bible, many of us immediately identify ourselves with the wrong person.

In Luke 15 Jesus tells the story we usually refer to as the parable of the prodigal son. In the story, one of the sons, the younger one, asks his dad to receive his inheritance early.

Culturally it would have been like saying, "Drop dead, Dad." Surprisingly the dad agrees, and with the money burning a hole in his pocket, the son immediately sets off for a distant country, where he squanders all his inheritance on wine and women. Devastated and destitute, he heads for the one place he never intended to be again: home. When the father sees him at a distance, he runs to him, puts his robe on him, and commands for the fattened calf to be killed. In other words, get out the party hats and kazoos; they were going to party like it was 1999, or something like that.

The father's response to the return of his wayward son was shocking. The same could be said about the older brother. His response was shocking, but in a very different way. You would expect that as the party began he would be the one offering a toast in honor of his returned brother. Instead, while the party raged on, he sat outside and pouted, and wondered why such a party had never been thrown for him.

Every time I have ever heard someone discuss that story, they identify themselves with the same character: the wayward son. Everyone, including me, has a story about how they wavered from God's plan, ran away, squandered something, and then came crawling back to God. If this story were turned into a stage production, all of us would try out for the part of the younger brother.

But really, and this is probably going to hurt a little, most of us would be more natural playing the role of the older brother.

Proud.

Self-righteous.

Nearsighted.

I would. I am not proud of this confession, but I am a recovering older brother. If "older brother" sounds like a sickness of some kind, it should. It is. Actually, being the "older brother" is just the symptom of the real sickness: religion.

I have digressed. My point is that most of us tend to identify ourselves with the wrong character when we study Bible stories.

The story of Hosea and Gomer is no different.

Most of us would say we are like Hosea—called by God to carry out a task. We do not necessarily understand the task, and may not even agree with it, but when God speaks, we listen, move, and obey.

So, we are like Hosea. Or so we think.

Let me be the bearer of bad news—or good news, depending upon how you take it. We are Gomer.

We are not the rescuer; we are the rescued.

We are not the redeemer; we are the redeemed.

We are not the lover; we are the loved. By God.

God loves us with an I-will-go-to-the-red-light-district-to-buy-them-back-from-their-sin love.

Or, I should say that God loves us with an I-will-go-to-a-red-bloodstained-cross-to-buy-them-back-from-their-sin love.

God loves us . . . undeservedly, recklessly, foolishly, shamelessly, furiously.

He is madly in love . . . with you, with me, with us. All of us.

He loves . . . the attractive, the rich, the sought after, the successful, the intelligent, the strong, the overlooked and undervalued, the poor, the marginalized, the weak, the frail, the discouraged.

The ones who know it. And the ones who don't.

God loves. He shows and he tells. And not only that, God is love.

When you are one of the few, the very few, who come to the stunning realization that you are liked (lyved) and loved by God, there is only one appropriate response. To love—God and others.

Madly.

As I have already told you, I grew up in a small Midwestern church, where we were hardcore Sunday-nighters. Sometimes on those Sunday nights we would have hymn-sings. I loved those nights. The song leader would take requests, and when I had the opportunity, I requested the same song almost every time. I would sing it for you, but you wouldn't be able to hear me. These are the words of the refrain:

> They will know we are Christians by our love, by our love
> Yes they'll know we are Christians by our love.

They should. But do they? They used to . . . the first church was saturated with love. For them, love was not a noun but a verb. They loved the attractive, rich, sought after, successful, intelligent, strong, the overlooked and undervalued, poor, marginalized, weak, frail, and discouraged.

Sound familiar? They loved. Like Jesus.

My sister, Jenni, is a missionary in a third-world Asian country. She works with an organization that protects and provides for young girls after they have been rescued from sex slavery, which unfortunately is an industry that is booming all over the world, especially in Asia. Several months ago I received an email from Jenni explaining she had learned that the mother of one of the young girls she works with had been admitted to the hospital. The woman was dying from complications related to having AIDS. Jenni visited the woman, and what she saw left her stunned and silent. The woman had shriveled down to skin and bones. Her once well-rounded cheeks had become craters. The woman's eyes, once bright and full of life, were clouded with an expression that said death was coming. She was so weak her words were barely audible, but even her silent expression was shouting for help.

You have to know that in the culture Jenni lives in, hospital patients may be given medicine, but they are not necessarily provided with meals or hygiene assistance. My sister couldn't stomach the idea of this dying woman also having to deal with hunger pangs and dirty undergarments, so each day she returned to the hospital to care for her. She took meals and washed clothes and changed undergarments. Also, the woman's young son sat next to the bed all day every day because he had no way to get to school, so Jenni started picking him up and giving him a ride to school, then she would take him back to the hospital after school and leave him with food for the night. She did this for weeks, doing whatever she could do to care for this woman and try to meet her needs. Several weeks later I received another email from my sister, and she shared that the woman, who lives in a land dominated by Buddhism, had surrendered her life to Jesus as Lord and Savior.

If you are like me, you hear stories like those and are tempted to say, "If I lived in a third-world country that is exactly how I would live too. I would be in the hospitals caring for patients, changing sheets, washing clothes, and sharing meals. I would always be looking for an opportunity to love like Jesus." And we would say this with the very best of intentions, but here is the reality: Most of us are probably never going to live in a third-world country. The real question is, are we committed to loving like Jesus in the midst of our everyday lives? It is easy to look at the circumstances of our lives and think, *If I had more time, then I would love like Jesus,* or *If I had a little extra discretionary income, then I would love like Jesus,* or *If I didn't have so many responsibilities already, then I would love like Jesus.*

Subconsciously, we can settle for an if/then mentality and never share love. Really, we need to shift from if/then to here/now. So no matter where you find yourself, it becomes *Right here, right now, I am going to love those who are in my circle of interaction and influence.* So who does that mean in your life?

Perhaps the person you need to intentionally love is the single mom at work who is always discouraged. You know just from listening to her conversations that she is working as hard as she can and yet struggling to make ends meet. The kids are having a difficult time dealing with Dad being gone, and they take out their hurt and pain on her. So not only has she been left alone, she has been left alone to raise children. When you pass each other in the hallways, she is always smiling on the outside, but on the inside she is crumbling to pieces.

Or the widowed woman who lives next door. Several years ago she buried her husband, but to her that seems like yesterday. You rarely see her garage door going up anymore because she hides behind the walls of her home, trapped in a cell of loneliness. In fact, the only time you see her is when she sneaks outside to grab the mail or makes a necessary trip to the grocery store.

Or maybe the person in your life in need of love is your boss at work. On the outside he has the perfect life. He drives a car worth as much as your house, dines at the finest restaurants in town, and is always dressed in designer suits. In his office you see pictures of a family—his wife and two cute kids—but you know that the only time he really "sees" them is when he looks up at those pictures. He is a workaholic, his identity is in his position, and he rationalizes to himself that one day things will slow down, but one day never seems to come.

I am sure that none of these descriptions fits exactly with people in your life, but I would guess that just hearing those descriptions reminded you of names and faces of people you do intersect with on a daily basis. So, no matter who you are, no matter what your life is like, every day you are surrounded by opportunities to feed, to encourage, to listen, to invest, to invite—all of them opportunities to love like Jesus. See, when talking about *loving like Jesus*, it's easy to think only in terms of starving people in other countries, or children who are sitting in orphanages around the world, or men and women in distant locations who do not have safe, clean drinking water. Certainly we should be dead serious about loving the overlooked and undervalued people all over this world, and there are numerous venues to do this. But loving like Jesus needs to happen in the here and now as well.

But what does loving like Jesus look like? There is too much at stake to just sit back and hope it happens, so the best way to understand his love is to peek into his life. Over these last several months, I have spent a great amount of time simply reading through the life of Jesus found in the Gospels, and as I read, I continually asked myself a couple of questions.

The first and most basic question is: **Whom did Jesus love?** This is the easiest to answer: everyone. I know that sounds like a churchy answer, but he really did love everyone. You find Jesus spending time with tax collectors and prostitutes, lepers and children, men and women, the religious and the irreligious, the wealthy and the poor . . . Jesus loved everyone. I suppose it would be easy to skip over this aspect of what it is to love like Jesus, but there are just some people we struggle to love. And if we were totally transparent, there is probably some type or category of people that is more difficult for each of us to love than others. At the same time, most of us have a category of people who is easy to love, and so when we intersect with someone in that group, we immediately find ways to love that person. Who is it for you?

Let me start.

The easiest people for me to love in practical ways are the ones living in the margins of society. So if I am downtown and run into a homeless person, I want to offer to buy a meal, a bottle of water, or to sit down and have a conversation. It is not like every single time I see a homeless person, I meet every need he or she has; that is not the point. I am simply saying that the down-and-outers of this world immediately get my attention; it is easy for me to love them. I don't tend to get wrapped up in why they are homeless, or what they should do so they are no longer homeless, or wonder about who's at fault. I just see someone who is homeless and my heart breaks, and I want to love them like Jesus would love them.

But let me also admit there is a type of people whom I struggle to love. Hear me out, because this is going to sound strange, I know, but the people I struggle with loving the most are the super-religious.

I have given you a glimpse into the spiritual environment of my childhood, but let me pull back the curtain a bit more. The church I attended was a super-religious one. It was not overly formal or ritualistic, but generally speaking, the greatest emphasis was placed on following a set of arbitrary rules. The whole premise of the faith was sin-avoidance. So if you stayed away from the supposedly big sins, and you showed up at church regularly, you had Christianity figured out. Because of this, we were not overly welcoming to outsiders. Whether new people came from another church setting or no church setting, they were likely not as successful as we were at following the arbitrary set of rules. So although we said our church was for everyone, it really wasn't. If you weren't adhering to the rules we all lived by, you were not going to feel very welcome.

I distinctly remember a time when one woman visited our church for the first time. She was obviously a chain smoker, because the smell of smoke followed her around. After church, she explained she needed a ride home. She lived quite a distance away, and she wondered if anyone could give her a ride. One family lived in the same direction, and I remember hearing them say in a hushed whisper that they were not willing to give her a ride because they didn't want their car to smell like smoke. That was the kind of spiritual environment I grew up in—surrounded by super-religious people who believed God's grace was good enough for them but not for anyone else.

Loving those people is hard for me. Come to find out, that makes me a lot like those people.

That is a peek into my life, but undoubtedly we all love the "easy" people and typically ignore the "difficult" ones. To the contrary, study Jesus' life and you will find he loved *everyone*.

So here is my challenge to you: Identify whom you struggle to love and find a way to love that person or group of people. Maybe you struggle to love illegal immigrants, or people in a conflicting political party, or people who are trapped in blatant sin, or people who are part of a different faith movement. Whoever it may be, love not in theory but in practicality. I know it is easier said than done. Trust me, I have failed to love like Jesus more times than I have followed through, but the times I have followed his leading have been some of the most pivotal, memorable moments of my life.

I wish I could tell you that every time you love a person like Jesus would they will fall in love with Jesus. Occasionally that will happen, but not always. Regardless, again, think about a person or group of people whom you struggle to love and find a practical way to share the love of Jesus with them. Perhaps it involves walking next door to your stubborn neighbor and delivering a meal, or signing up to volunteer at a refugee center. Committing to love like Jesus loves might mean you invest yourself in a community of people who doesn't look like you, act like you, or talk like you. No matter the specifics, find practical ways to love people like Jesus would love them—and not just the easy people, but the difficult people.

The first question I asked as I read through Jesus' life and ministry was "Whom did he love?" and the answer is "everyone," but the second question I wrestled with was . . .

How did Jesus love? I will answer with one word: intentionally. There were plenty of times when people would come to Jesus hungry, or thirsty, or sick, or lonely, and he would meet their needs. In a sense, he showed his love reactively. But more often than not, he loved people proactively. By that I mean he sought out opportunities to express his love for people in practical ways.

In John 4 we find the familiar story of Jesus and the Samaritan woman at the well. In those days, it was culturally unacceptable for Jesus to talk to this Samaritan woman in public, because (1) she was a Samaritan and (2) she was a woman. Jews and Samaritans did not associate with each other. The Jews perceived the Samaritans as something less than fully human; they were kind of the scum of the earth. Also, in that day men did not associate with women in public. For these reasons and more, it would have gone against the culture for Jesus to speak a word to her. But Jesus knew she was hurting and desperately in need. See, Jesus knew the woman had had several husbands already and now was living with another man who was not her husband. We do not know all the details, but we know enough to conclude that she was broken, lonely, and an outcast in the eyes of her friends, family, and neighbors. Even if their paths would have crossed by accident, it was a display of extravagant love that he initiated an in-depth conversation with her in public about life and love and faith, but we know their meeting was not accidental.

The story starts by telling us this about Jesus: "Now he had to go through Samaria" (John 4:4). Note the phrase "had to." If you don't understand those words, you cannot understand this passage. There was a well-traveled path that went around Samaria. It was well traveled for a reason; no Jew worth his salt would have willingly traveled into Samaria, especially when there was a clear-cut alternative route. So Jesus' GPS could have taken him a different way, but his heart demanded he go through Samaria. Bottom line, Jesus didn't accidentally run into this broken, lonely woman at the well in Samaria; he intentionally chose an itinerary that led him right to her.

Most of the time loving like Jesus is going to happen as you travel the path of your daily life, and that path will be saturated with opportunities. But there will be times when we have to intentionally set a course that will lead us to love people like Jesus would love them.

There is a group of women at the church I serve who could easily be mistaken for Jesus because of the way they love. They love everyone. Intentionally.

Recently they learned about an organization in downtown Cincinnati that works with recovering prostitutes. Immediately they wanted to get involved. They wanted to love. So they drove downtown to the rehab center, ordered pizzas, and spent an evening talking, laughing, dancing, and praying with women who have been living in the trap of prostitution. The women of our church traveled down there intentionally, for one reason: to *love like Jesus*. John 4 says Jesus had to travel through Samaria. I think our women would tell you, "We had to travel to downtown Cincinnati." When loving like Jesus is the mission and purpose of your life, there are going to be times when you travel way off the beaten path; it will almost feel like you have to, but it won't be a have-to obligation. It will be a have-to opportunity you wouldn't miss for the world, an opportunity to love like Jesus.

Whether on the path you walk every day or a path that is less traveled, loving like Jesus happens intentionally. To love like Jesus loves is to love everyone: irresponsibly, recklessly, foolishly, endlessly, indiscriminately, and intentionally.

But God demonstrates his own love for us in this: While we were still sinners, Christ died for us.

Romans 5:8

For God so loved the world that he gave his one and only Son, that whoever believes in him shall not perish but have eternal life.

John 3:16

This life of love we are called to is patterned after Jesus, who walked a road less traveled—a road that led to a cross. He was not forced to die on a cross, he did not accidentally die on a cross; he intentionally died on a cross.

That's love. Mad love.

The story of Jesus, from the wooden manger to the wooden cross, is the story of a God who has gone to all lengths to show and tell his people that they are loved. Despite this truth, many people still do not know they are loved. Evidence for that statement is hard to miss.

Glance around your town or neighborhood and you will undoubtedly find that racism is alive and well, hatred is rampant, dissension is the norm, divorce is not only accepted but expected, the black clouds of terrorism are always looming, and infectious diseases are on the loose. I am not trying to be like Chicken Little, saying, "The sky is falling, the sky is falling!" but just take an honest inventory of our world. The picture is pretty bleak.

At the risk of oversimplifying the situation, there is a cure for the world's ailments: love. Now, understand, I am not a tree-hugging, tie-dye-wearing, pot-smoking hippie from the sixties who thinks love is the answer to every question. I am saying that if tomorrow morning every man, woman, and child on planet earth woke up convinced they are loved by the Almighty God, every war would end, abuse would halt, addictions would be no more, insecurities would be swept away, anger would dissolve, fears would subside, and conflict would be resolved. That is what God's love does.

People just need to be shown and told.

By you. By me. By us.

Yes, they are loved. Madly.

And if you are serious about showing and telling the love of Jesus, you might find yourself in the midst of some dark, dirty, disgusting places like a red-light district.

Yes, we are Gomer. And Hosea.

⌐ Reflection/Discussion ⌐

1. Read through Hosea in the Old Testament and try to fathom the intense love required for Hosea to buy Gomer back from prostitution. Then spend time considering the implications in regard to God's love for you.

2. Consider the faith gathering you are part of (if you are part of one). Do people know you by the way you love people? If not, how would you say you are known in your community or neighborhood at large? Be honest.

3. What changes need to be made at a corporate or personal level that would allow you to be known by your love?

4. What circumstances of your life seem like obstacles to loving like Jesus? What changes can you make to those circumstances to remove the obstacles? If the circumstances are not changeable, search for ways to love practically in spite of the circumstances.

⌐ Prayer ⌐

Father, teach us to live in a way that we will be known for our love. Give us eyes to recognize the opportunities that surround us. When there seem to be obstacles, teach us how to love through them or in the midst of them. More than anything, teach us to grasp the depth and width of the love you have for us, that we would learn to love others in the same manner. Thank you for loving us so recklessly, unconditionally, and endlessly. Your love changes everything. In Jesus' name.

Part Three

The **real** Answer

13

Brushstrokes

Unbridled generosity.
  Daring courage.
  Rebellious joy.
  Risky faith.
  Relentless hope.
  Scandalous grace.
  Mad love.

  Independently, these attributes do not have much value. The same could be said about one brushstroke alone on a canvas. But when all of these brushstrokes are put on a canvas together, they form a portrait that is not still, stagnant, or static, but is moving, acting, and breathing.

  The portrait is of Jesus.

  Now, understand that these brushstrokes do not in any way paint a *complete* portrait of Jesus, for that would be impossible to do with words. But at some level they do serve as a self-portrait of Jesus, or at least that is my intention.

  See, we have not been called to emulate a picture, as beautiful as it may be, but a person.

Jesus.

During Jesus' ministry, he said, "Be like me, act like me, live like me, laugh like me, and love like me." You won't find Jesus saying these exact words in the Gospels, but he implied them all and so much more every time he said, "Follow me."

We spoke earlier about how the call to pick up a cross has gotten lost in translation. The same is true for the initial command Jesus gave his first followers—and ultimately us: "Follow me."

We use those same words today, but without Jesus' intent. For example, when someone walks into our church building for the first time and asks, "Where is the children's ministry area?" I say, "Follow me." And after walking down the hall and down the steps, we quickly arrive at our destination. We exchange pleasantries, and the act of following is over. Our "follow me" invitation implies a rather simple, often quite short, journey. A stroll in the hallway. A cruise on the highway. A hop, skip, and a jump through the backyard.

Following someone now is usually safe, quick, and usually involves very little investment, thought, or effort.

Not so when following Jesus. That is, if we are serious about following him.

Unfortunately, many seem to think that following Jesus is a part-time gig. They sign up on a whim and barely give it a second thought. Jesus warned against such frivolous decision making:

> Suppose one of you wants to build a tower. Won't you first sit down and estimate the cost to see if you have enough money to complete it? For if you lay the foundation and are not able to finish it, everyone who sees it will ridicule you, saying, "This person began to build and was not able to finish."
>
> Luke 14:28–30

The decision to build a tower is a calculated one. You don't wander your way into that decision or make it casually. The word *estimate* originally meant "to count with pebbles." The original word indicated a meticulous reckoning of the specific cost. As opposed to a mere estimation, estimate indicated an explicit calculation.

> Or suppose a king is about to go to war against another king. Won't he first sit down and consider whether he is able with ten thousand men to oppose the one coming against him with twenty thousand? If he is not able, he will send a delegation while the other is still a long way off and will ask for terms of peace.
>
> Luke 14:31–32

The crowd surrounding Jesus wouldn't have had any difficulty clearly understanding his message.

If you are going to build a tower, you'd better count your money.

If you are going to war, you'd better count your soldiers.

And in the same way, if you are going to set out following Jesus, you'd better count the cost.

Following Jesus *is* a costly decision. It costs everything. So the first question to consider is, "Is it worth the cost to be a disciple of Jesus?" This is not a rhetorical question for any of us.

The question demands an answer, and by the way, not answering is an answer. The question is difficult because of the word *disciple*, which isn't used in everyday language. In fact, it is practically nonexistent within our language and conversation, which means we are left to answer a question that we do not even fully understand. Perhaps that is why so many sign up to be a disciple of Jesus on a whim without calculating the costs.

Only when you study the first-century relationship between

rabbi and disciple does the high cost of discipleship become evident. Interestingly enough, one title for Jesus in the Gospels was rabbi.

In the first century, rabbis who taught the Torah were some of the most admired members of the community. They were the brightest students; they were experts in the Law. They were few and far between.

Jewish children began their schooling at an early age, and from the beginning their goal was to become a disciple of a rabbi. And so they involved themselves in incredibly intense processes of learning God's Word. The students began their schooling by memorizing the Torah, which is the first five books of the Bible. History tells us most students would have the entire section memorized by the age of ten. That's Genesis, Exodus, Leviticus, Numbers, and Deuteronomy. All memorized. (So maybe a Sunday school verse here and there isn't that difficult after all.) Around the same age, the brighter students began to separate themselves from the others and continued along the lines of education in hopes of following a rabbi later in life. A great portion of their continued education was Scripture memorization. Not just some Scripture, but all Scripture. By the age of thirteen or fourteen, the best students had all thirty-nine books of the Old Testament memorized word for word.

Genesis to Malachi. Memorized.

By his late teens, a student who was qualified to do so would approach a chosen rabbi and say, "Rabbi, I want to become one of your disciples." When a student sought to follow a rabbi, he was hoping to take on the rabbi's yoke—the system of beliefs and interpretations the rabbi had either developed or carried on from previous generations.

By the way, it was only every once in a while that a rabbi would come along and teach a new yoke. Most rabbis would preach a yoke of somebody else, just quoting the thoughts of others. So the rabbi would come along and say, "I am teaching the yoke of so and so," and if that interested the people, they would listen. But nothing was more appealing to a crowd or to a student than when a rabbi came and taught a new yoke of his own. When a rabbi preached his own yoke, it was said that he taught with authority. Sound familiar? At the end of the Sermon on the Mount, we are told the crowds were astonished because Jesus taught with authority like they had never seen. Jesus came with his own yoke.

I suppose you wouldn't expect the Son of God to borrow someone else's material.

When a rabbi came with a new yoke, people would do anything to listen to their teaching. They would walk for miles on end until they ran out of food and water and wound up in the middle of who knows where, all for the chance to hear the rabbi teach. They would sit for hours on a mountainside or even tear a roof off of someone's house to get close enough to hear.

So when a prospective student approached a rabbi, he had to make a decision to either accept or reject the request. The rabbi's fundamental driving question is, "Does this student have what it takes?" "Can this student be like me?" "Does this student have what it takes to do what I do?"

To test the kid's ability and knowledge, the rabbi would question the student. Not just *a* question. Many questions—questions that would help determine if the student knew the text inside and out like the rabbi did. It was not enough to have the words, phrases, and passages memorized. More important, "Does the student understand the implications of the words, phrases, and passages?" The questions were not for the faint of heart; they were designed to separate the men from the boys. Actually, the boys from the boys, but you know what I mean.

And after putting the student through a series of tests, if the rabbi thought he had what it took, the rabbi would simply say, "Come, follow me."

If you were accepted to be a disciple, you would then as a teenager leave your parents and brothers and sisters, your synagogue, your school, and even your friends. With no hesitation, you would leave everything familiar and devote your entire life to being like your rabbi. Everything your rabbi did, you would do. If your rabbi was walking along and picked up a blade of grass and ate it, you would pick up a blade of grass and put it in your mouth. There was nothing he did that you would not do. Some historians even say disciples would go into the restroom with their rabbi so that they didn't miss out on anything.

I think some things are worth missing.

For disciples, great sacrifice was always involved when they chose to follow a rabbi. It required total surrender. I have heard it said that partial surrender is no surrender at all. Following the rabbi became the student's only priority. Their relationship was defined by complete and total commitment. It was a costly decision.

Everything.

Following Jesus is not a sometimes thing; following Him is an all-the-time thing.

All day.

Every day.

When you follow Jesus, and follow him closely, there are certainly going to be some attributes that become evident in your life. However, those attributes are not the goal of following Jesus, they are the fruit of following Jesus. Or let me say it like this, they are indications that one is following after Jesus. With that said, do not fall for the common trap of thinking that following Jesus can be reduced down to a list. Following Jesus cannot be captured by or reduced down to a list of rules, a list of behaviors, or even a list of attributes, as admirable or holy as they may be.

We must get this: Christianity is not about following a list, a creed, or a mere doctrine. It is about following a real man named Jesus.

On Sunday.

And Monday through Saturday.

⌐ Reflection/Discussion ⌐

1. If you were to paint a portrait of Jesus, what attributes would be used?

2. In your own words, what is implied when Jesus says, "Follow me"? What does a life of following Jesus look like in our twenty-first-century context?

3. What obstacles, if any, hinder you the most from following Jesus well? Fear? Comfort? Uncertainty? Complacency?

4. Have you ever actually considered the costs of following Jesus? Or is it possible you wandered into this life without giving it proper consideration?

⌐ Prayer ⌐

Father, thank you for inviting us to follow you. For the times and the ways we have settled for something less than following you, please forgive us. Continue to teach us how to live and how to love as you would. There is great cost in following you, but the rewards are much greater—in this life and the life to come. Constantly remind us not to settle for following a list of rules, or a creed, or a specific tradition, but only to be content following you. In Jesus' name.

14

Good News

When Jesus finally began his earthly ministry, around the age of thirty, he immediately began preaching and teaching. As the Son of God, you might expect that his messages were laced with complex theology. Instead, his teachings were quite simple. His message could be well summarized this way: "The kingdom of God has come near. Repent and believe the good news!" (Mark 1:14–15). So much for three-point sermons or annoyingly artistic alliteration. Jesus was a one-point preacher.

Everywhere Jesus traveled throughout his three-year ministry, he taught good news. As you may know, the word *gospel* means "good news." Not only did Jesus teach good news, he *was* good news to people. Throughout the gospel accounts you find Jesus feeding the hungry, taking care of the poor, restoring dignity to the marginalized people of society, and casting out evil spirits. His life and ministry creates a great model for us as his followers.

Following Jesus is not so much about following him in a directional sense, like east or west on a path, but more about getting wrapped up in the things he is wrapped up in. So following Jesus has less to do with whether you go here, there, or somewhere else, and more about being good news to people here, there, or somewhere else.

Are you good news to the people around you, those within your circle of influence? This is a question I ask myself regularly. Sometimes I am happy with my answer and sometimes I am not. Now back to you: Again, are you good news to the people within your circle of influence?

When I talk about being good news to people, I mean infusing hope and joy and peace and patience and kindness and self-control and love into the daily circumstances of this world. In many ways, we cannot dictate those circumstances, but we can absolutely decide how we affect the circumstances. When people are around you, are they inclined to be anxious and uptight? Or is there something about your natural disposition that ushers peace into the hearts and minds of people? When you are involved in a conversation, is it common for the tone to become testy and condescending? Or do you create a tone that allows for honest dialogue void of defensive or offensive statements? When someone has stumbled into sin, would they be inclined to confide in you, knowing they will encounter loving truth? Or are they more likely to hide the sin from you, knowing you would speak harsh words of judgment?

Certainly these questions are not an exhaustive evaluation of whether or not you are good news to the people around you, but if you are like me, honestly dealing even with these few questions seems a bit exhausting.

Are you good news to people? None of us are Jesus reincarnate. Therefore none of us will always be good news to everyone we encounter. However, do not allow that obvious reality to deter you from answering the question in general terms. Along the path of life are you good news?

As I reflect on my adolescent years, unfortunately I recognize that at many times and in many ways I was not good news. I have briefly shared with you the kind of spiritual environment I grew up in. Needless to say, it was not necessarily the good-news type. I followed suit. When I was in junior and senior high I wore the same outfit to school almost every single day—a long black robe—and I carried a gavel in my hand. I was a little Judge Wapner in disguise. (If you are under thirty, you have no idea who Judge Wapner is. He was the Judge Judy of the eighties. This is getting confusing.) Suffice it to say, I was judge and jury of anyone and everyone I encountered.

For years I equated following Jesus with following an arbitrary set of rules, so judgments were easy to make. Follow the same rules I did, or else. Sometimes I was bold enough to be outspoken in my judgment. Many times, however, the judgment would happen within the courtroom of my own mind. Either way I was definitely keeping track. So as I listened to conversations at school about the latest drunken party or newly released R-rated movie that everyone else was going to see, I was privately, sometimes publicly, banging the gavel of judgment.

There is one particular moment I do not think I will ever be able to erase from my memory. Honestly, I wish I could. There was a young man in my English Composition class whose father tragically took his own life. As a member of our school's ensemble choir, I even sang at his father's funeral. Several weeks after my classmate had returned to school, I remember the issue of suicide coming up in conversation. Totally oblivious to the young man sitting in the circle who had just lost his father to suicide, I went on a tirade about how someone who committed suicide could never enter heaven. In all my glory, I explained how anyone who committed suicide had given up both on themselves and on God, so why would God allow them to be in heaven. Even now, as I reflect back on that moment, I have tears in the corners of my eyes and a knot in my stomach. If Jesus had been in that room, he would have embraced my classmate as soon as the conversation about suicide began, all while I was lost in a tirade about how suicide was a one-way ticket to hell.

I am ashamed to say it, but in many ways during that season of my life, I was not good news.

Over the years, as I have been washed in God's grace, I would like to think I have become good news to the people in my circle of influence. I am continuing to learn that when I am good news to people, I am given the opportunity to share the good news with people. Even when the opportunity to teach good news does not come, we are still called to be good news.

Are you good news? Take some time to reflect on the relationships you are involved in. Think about co-workers, neighbors, and relatives. Are you good news to them?

As you consider this question, you may start to become more equipped to determine whether you are following Jesus or just showing up at a building on a certain day every week. Perhaps Sunday.

⌐— Reflection/Discussion —⌐

1. After you honestly evaluate your life, answer this question: Are you good news to the people within your circle of influence?

2. Talk about the times you have admittedly failed to be good news. What lessons can you learn about those experiences?

3. Being good news often requires intentional effort. As you evaluate your life, what effort could you make to be good news to those around you?

4. Talk about the people in your life whom you would consider to be good news. What about their life would cause you to label them this way? Talk about specific examples.

⌐ Prayer ⌐

Father, as we journey through life, give us the wisdom and courage to be good news to those we encounter. Let our lifestyle and interaction with others match the message we share. When we fail, teach us to be humble enough to repent. Thank you for modeling what a life of good news looks like. In Jesus' name.

15

Duct Tape

Have you ever noticed that you can be in any section of a big-box home improvement store like Home Depot or Lowe's, and within ten feet there is always a rack of duct tape? You can be in the paint section, the lawn mower section, the pipe section, the lumber section, or even the home and garden section, and you are always just a few steps away from a roll of duct tape. There is a subliminal message.

Duct tape fixes everything.

You would think most people would realize that duct tape cannot really fix everything, and that is probably true.

I am not most people.

About two years ago, my wife, Alex, and I pulled into our driveway late one night and I noticed that our mailbox was no longer attached to its post. This was not shocking news. Apparently some kids in our neighborhood were fascinated with knocking down mailboxes, because this happened to us all the time. So even though it was late, I did what the man of the house has to do, and I made a beeline for the tool section of our garage. Just to be clear, when I say the "tool section," I mean a Tupperware container that holds my tools. By the way, I don't care what my wife says, just because Tonka is the maker of my tools, it doesn't mean they are not real tools. Honestly, I do have some nice tools in there, but the first two tools I grab for any job are the superglue and the duct tape. So that night I took a tube of superglue and a roll of duct tape out to the street with me, and in a matter of five minutes I had that mailbox taped back to the pole. That may sound like a temporary fix, but I am proud to say my mailbox was duct taped for almost a year. I did have to re-tape it every week or two, but like most men, I love any opportunity to use my favorite tool, so I didn't mind at all.

Here is my personal philosophy: Anything that duct tape can't fix, more duct tape can. I take that back. There *are* some things duct tape can't fix. Just ask my wife.

If we are honest about twenty-first-century American Christianity, we have an issue that goes back to the discussion that began this book: a Sunday-centric faith. Again, not everyone has settled for a Sunday-centric faith, but I think it affects more of us than we care to admit. And duct tape won't fix it.

The fact is, there are no easy ways to reverse the trend of living and passing on Sunday-centric faith. Many of us do not even recognize the behavior because it comes so natural to us; sadly, it may be the only thing we know.

If you have settled for, or been lulled into, a Sunday-centric faith— intentionally or unintentionally—do not worry, do not fret, do not be too hard on yourself. None of these is the appropriate response, but there is one.

In the book of Revelation, we find seven letters to seven churches. John may have written Revelation, but Jesus wrote these letters. I said that once on a Sunday morning, and someone scolded me in the lobby for speaking figuratively. If you are scolding me right now, I am sorry. But Jesus wrote the letters.

Anyway, in every one of the letters, Jesus, in a sense, put the church under a microscope to diagnose their condition. (There I go using figurative language again.)

> To the angel of the church in Ephesus write:
> There are the words of him who holds the seven stars in his right hand and walks among the seven golden lampstands. I know your deeds, your hard work and your perseverance. I know that you cannot tolerate wicked people, that you have tested those who claim to be apostles but are not, and have found them false. You have persevered and have endured hardships for my name, and have not grown weary.
>
> Revelation 2:1–3

As Jesus begins his diagnosis of the Ephesian church, all seems to be well. It is obvious from his words that they are not turning their eye away from sin; they were addressing it head-on. When the culture at large was letting truth become a relative idea, they continued to cling to absolute truth. These people were pressing on in the face of persecution; they continued running even after they had hit the wall. In these first few sentences, the church is getting a five-star review; they are getting two thumbs up from Jesus. Then comes verses 4 and 5. Apparently, just below the church's surface, there is a significant problem:

> Yet I hold this against you: You have forsaken the love you had at first. Consider how far you have fallen!

According to Jesus, the Ephesian church had lost their first love. Some believe this to mean they had stopped loving people. Others, like me, think the church had stopped loving Jesus. Either way, the effect is the same. I mean, if you stop loving people, you also stop loving Jesus. You understand that, right?

Loving others isn't optional in the Christian life. It seems like some people think that actively and practically loving others is a spiritual gift you either have or you don't. So if you don't have the gift, it's fine, because someone else does. That is not how it works.

Anyway, somehow, someway the Ephesian church had lost their first love. I am confident it didn't happen intentionally. Just like in a marriage, people do not usually intentionally fall out of love, but it happens all the time. It is often a slow but steady fade . . . and love gets forsaken.

Losing our first love for Christ can mean a lot of different things and look different in a lot of ways. For instance, settling for a Sunday-centric faith.

As Jesus continued his letter to the Ephesians, he clearly instructed them on how to respond in light of having lost their first love.

Repent.

Often people think about repentance in terms of being a threat. It is not. It is an invitation.

To turn back.

To start again.

To be made whole and new and right.

So if you have settled for a Sunday-centric faith, Jesus is not looming over you with a clenched fist. Instead, he is standing with open arms, inviting you back.

The appropriate response when we recognize a Sunday-centric faith in ourselves is to repent, but how do we stop this kind of faith being perpetuated to others? In other words, how do we stop the vicious cycle?

I only have one suggestion. For some it is going to sound absurd; others will get it. Here it is:

Stop inviting people to church. On Sunday.

I know how crazy that may seem. I am a pastor of a church, and we are constantly encouraging our people to invite, invite, invite. Bring, bring, bring.

People.

To church.

On Sunday.

Obviously there is value in inviting people to come to church with you on Sunday (or Saturday). But when the invitation always begins with simply showing up at a building on Sunday, it is natural for that to become the foundation on which one's faith is built. Or better said, all too easily the time spent in that building on that day can become the axis on which their new faith will spin.

It is also tempting to invite someone to show up at a place and then believe our work is done. That is partly how, as a church, we have lost perspective when it comes to the clergy/laity issue. In Bible times there were no clergy or laity, there were just Christians. And all of them were sent into the world to share the gospel message of Jesus Christ crucified and resurrected to life for us. As followers of Jesus we have all been sent.

Inviting people to come to church is a back-door way of introducing people to Jesus, but what if we just went through the front door? What if we first invited them to follow a person? Jesus.

One of the most overlooked disciples is Andrew. That should come as no surprise; his brother was Peter, who lived in the limelight.

Peter preached the first gospel sermon on the day of Pentecost.

Peter denied Jesus three times before the rooster crowed.

Peter was referred to as Satan, by Jesus.

Peter initially refused to let Jesus wash his feet, then begged him for a full-body sponge bath.

Peter was always holding the microphone; he always lived in the limelight—sometimes for the good, many times for the bad.

Andrew did not. In fact Andrew is almost never mentioned, but the few times he is, we are told he was doing the same thing: bringing someone to Jesus.

Interestingly enough, the first person Andrew brought to Jesus was Peter. In John 1, we see that one day John the Baptist was with two of his disciples when Jesus passed by. John said, "Look, the Lamb of God!" When Andrew and the other disciple heard this, they followed Jesus to the place he had been staying and spent the day with him. Afterward, the first thing Andrew did was tell his brother Simon (Peter), "We have found the Messiah." John 1:42 says, "And he brought him to Jesus."

Andrew was also there when Jesus fed the five thousand. Earlier Jesus had tested his disciples by asking, "Where shall we buy bread for these people to eat?" Philip said, "Eight months wages would not buy enough bread for each one to have one bite!" Philip failed the test. But not Andrew.

> Another of his disciples, Andrew, Simon Peter's brother, spoke up, "Here is a boy with five small barley loaves and two small fish, but how far will they go among so many?"
>
> John 6:8–9

Andrew didn't know how the story would play out—how could he have possibly known? Yet here he was, bringing someone (in this instance, the boy) to Jesus.

Now, I want to be careful to be a good student of God's Word and not make it say something it does not say. So let's be clear. I am not suggesting there is a hidden "Andrew theology" that only I know about. However, I do contend that one way or another, Andrew was always connecting people with Jesus.

In John 12, there were some Greek people whom Philip met who wanted to see Jesus. What Philip does next is interesting. You would expect him to go to Jesus to talk about these Greeks.

Instead he went to Andrew, and together they went to Jesus. Why did Philip go to Andrew? Again, I don't want to read something into the text that is not there. However, at some level it is clear that Philip went to Andrew first because Andrew was always connecting people with Jesus. He may have lived in the shadow of his brother—in fact he is almost always referred to as Peter's brother. But Andrew lived to get people to Jesus as quickly as he could.

I cannot help but wonder what would happen if we modeled Andrew's approach? That instead of inviting people to a place—hoping through the music or a lesson or the sermon they will be introduced to Jesus—we instead got people to Jesus as quickly as possible?

What I am asking is, if instead of introducing people to the bride and hoping they meet the groom, what if we introduced people to the groom first?

I confess that many times I do just the opposite. Even though I know better, I am inclined to invite people to a program, or an activity, or a certain worship service instead of simply having a conversation about Jesus.

There is so much talk about how we have to first earn the right to be heard before we can share spiritual truths with people. *Really?* Or is that just a well-articulated excuse? Although I suppose I understand the logic behind it, this approach to evangelism seems to lack an appropriate urgency.

Andrew didn't waste any time earning the right to be heard; he got people to Jesus as quickly as possible.

When we seek to follow Jesus closely, and through the Holy Spirit live a life defined by . . .

Unbridled joy,
Daring courage,
Rebellious joy,
Risky faith,

Relentless hope,

Scandalous grace,

and mad love, people are inevitably going to look and listen. When they take notice of you as a result of your lifestyle, opportunities will arise to share conversation that could end in an invitation.

Not to church, but to Jesus.

On its own, leading people directly to Jesus will not eradicate the epidemic of Sunday-centric faith that already exists, but doing so has the potential to start reversing the tide. If we lead people to a faith that begins spinning on the axis of Jesus, likely the faith will continue that way. However, once people begin a life of faith that spins on an experience that happens at a place, on a certain day of the week, centrifugal force is hard to stop.

⌐ Reflection/Discussion ⌐

1. Discuss ways to lead people to Jesus without teaching them to settle for a Sunday faith.

2. What are possible ways to fix, change, or reverse the current trend of Sunday-centric faith that is alive and well?

3. Talk about Andrew and his habit of taking people directly to Jesus. Then evaluate your life and determine people you could potentially introduce to Jesus. Think in terms of specific names and faces.

4. Do you agree with the idea that you have to earn the right to be heard in terms of sharing Jesus with someone? Why or why not?

⌐ Prayer ⌐

Father, give us wisdom on how to reverse the reality of Sunday-centric faith. Teach us to value the corporate worship opportunities in life without building our faith on them. Also, Lord, teach us how to find a balance between inviting people to join us as we attend church and directly speaking to people about Jesus. So often we miss opportunities to speak directly about you. Help us to recognize the opportunities when they exist and give us the words to say when they do. In Jesus' name.

16

Glass

Glass is versatile. As I sit here at my desk, I am surrounded by glass; not literally, that would be strange, but figuratively. On the wall, on the door, on my desk. Beside me, in front of me, next to me. Glass is everywhere. It is one of the realities of life we likely don't pay much attention to, but it is everywhere, all of the time. Vain people tend to notice glass more often because it always offers one more opportunity to catch a glimpse of themselves. But whether you notice it or not, we are constantly surrounded by glass. It is used in cars, and homes, and restaurants, and stadiums, and parks. It comes in different shapes and sizes and colors.

Glass has two primary purposes: to be looked through and to be looked into.

Window versus mirror. One is to be looked through; the other is to be looked into. Both allow us to peek, gaze, and stare at reality. Yet they present two different realities.

A window allows you an escape. A departure. A distraction. A respite from your own reality.

I remember looking through a window from my hotel room high above Times Square. Several stories below there were yellow cabs, and bright lights, and people of every color and shape. In Miami, I once spent hours gazing through a floor-to-ceiling window at the breathtaking, crystal-colored ocean. When I write, I often look out the window of my office, and there is a dead bush. Yes, some windows are better than others, but all are portals to a new reality.

Then there are mirrors. Mirrors create opportunities to study your own reality, whether you like it or not. When you look into a mirror, nothing is hidden. If you are really brave, look into one of those magnifying mirrors. Everything is exposed: scars, cracks, crevices, wrinkles, pimples, every follicle of soft hair, and every rigid whisker.

Some love what they see in the mirror, others loathe it. Either way, a mirror offers an unfiltered glimpse of the reality of you.

As you have read about . . .

Unbridled generosity,

Daring courage,

Rebellious joy,

Risky faith,

Relentless hope,

Scandalous grace,

and mad love, have you been looking through a window at other people's lives? Or has it been more like looking in a mirror and recognizing your own life?

Window? Mirror? Little of both?

Window. If you have read through these pages and it felt like you were mainly gazing through a window at other people's lives, it would be . . .

a bad sign,

a red flag,

a warning light,

something much worse.

You cannot follow Jesus closely and not have even a hint of these attributes alive and well in your life. Or to continue the analogy I began a few chapters ago, if these seven brushstrokes of a 24/7 follower of Christ (unbridled generosity, daring courage, and the others) are not noticeable in your own self-portrait, perhaps you are not emulating the person of Jesus.

Mirror. If you have read through these pages and it felt like you were only looking in a mirror, it would be a . . .

a bad sign,

a red flag,

a warning light,

something much worse.

Hopefully you did find yourself in this portrait, but if you saw yourself on every line of every page, I'm not sure how honest you are being. Not with me, but with yourself. In the Christian life, it is when you feel like you have arrived or have it all figured out that you are in trouble for sure.

So how can you know if you have lost perspective as you read the Bible? How do you know if you are overestimating yourself? Answer: When you find yourself always agreeing with Jesus.

I know how crazy that must sound. Sacrilegious even. Aren't we supposed to agree with Jesus? Yes. But in this context, when I say "agree with Jesus," it is a perspective issue. Let me explain it like this.

Jesus tells a story about a Pharisee and a tax collector who are both at the temple praying:

> Two men went up to the temple to pray, one a Pharisee and the other a tax collector. The Pharisee stood by himself and prayed: "God, I thank you that I am not like other people—robbers, evildoers, adulterers—or even like this tax collector. I fast twice a week and give a tenth of all I get."

But the tax collector stood at a distance. He would not even look up to heaven, but beat his breast and said, "God, have mercy on me, a sinner."

I tell you that this man, rather than the other, went home justified before God. For all those who exalt themselves will be humbled, and those who humble themselves will be exalted.

Luke 18:10–14

If we are honest, many of us are thinking right now, *I am glad I am not like that religious leader.* Ironic, don't you think? In thanking God that we are not like the religious leader, we are like the religious leader.

This is just an example of how, in Scripture, if we are not careful, we can approach it as if it is never about us.

For the word of God is alive and active. Sharper than any double-edged sword, it penetrates even to dividing soul and spirit, joints and marrow; it judges the thoughts and attitudes of the heart.

Hebrews 4:12

The Word of God is sharp. Like a sword. Like a scalpel. It separates joints and marrow. The Word of God does spiritual surgery on its readers.

Surgery is painful. It hurts. It is necessary, but it is not often enjoyable. Like Jesus' words, they are necessary but not always enjoyable. He is speaking them because they still need to be heard—and not by someone else.

By me.

By you.

So when Jesus speaks, if you are always nodding your head and smiling, it is a sign that you think Jesus is only talking to someone else or doing surgery on someone else. He is not. People don't nod and smile when they are having surgery done.

Hopefully as you read through these attributes and studied this portrait, you felt like you were looking through a window and into a mirror at the same time. A little of both.

My hope is that you have found glimpses of yourself in these pages, and yet also realized there is still more room to grow, more to learn, more transformation to experience. A disciple who follows a rabbi always has more to learn. Especially when the rabbi is named Jesus. And he is the Christ.

If you read through the pages of the Bible, especially the teachings of Jesus, and feel like you fall short or don't measure up, do not become discouraged. Be encouraged. You are a work in progress. So am I. And our master designer never leaves a work undone.

> He who began a good work in you will carry it on to completion until the day of Christ Jesus.
>
> Philippians 1:6

In the meantime, keep staring through the window of Scripture, and if you allow the Holy Spirit to have his way in you, you will increasingly notice your reflection.

⌐ Reflection/Discussion ⌐

1. As you studied through the attributes of a 24/7 follower of Christ, were you looking through a window or into a mirror? Be specific.

2. Which attributes seem to be evident in your life? Which attributes are less evident or nonexistent in your life?

3. As you study Scripture, do you perceive Jesus always talking to other people? Or when you study do you feel like

you are having spiritual surgery performed on you? As you study the Bible, realize that Jesus is teaching you, not just others.

4. Talk about specific areas of your life where you need to experience growth in terms of following Jesus closely.

⌐ Prayer ⌐

Father, thank you for the power of your Word. Your words are not always comfortable or easy to study, but they are transformative. Thank you for the promise that you will complete the work of transformation that you have begun in us through the person and power of your Holy Spirit. Continually make us aware of areas of our lives that need to experience transformation. As we identify those areas, nudge us to resign ourselves to your way. In Jesus' name.

17

Final Answer

When the TV show *Who Wants to Be a Millionaire?* was introduced years ago, I thought it was a silly name. Who *doesn't* want to be a millionaire? The trivia game show was originally hosted by Regis Philbin, who holds the record for the most live time on television in American history. That information is worth what you paid for it.

Every contestant had an opportunity to win one million dollars, hence the name. To do so, the contestant simply had to answer fourteen consecutive multiple-choice questions correctly. Come to find out, it wasn't so simple. A few did, but very few. Obviously, the questions became increasingly difficult as each round passed and as the prize money grew. Every time a contestant would give their answer, Regis would ask the rhetorical question: "Is that your final answer?"

With the one-hundred- and two-hundred-dollar questions, contestants would usually answer with little thought. However, their demeanor changed, and rightly so, if they were fortunate enough to reach the million-dollar question. They would be noticeably nervous. Taking deeper breaths. Squirming a bit in the seat. When they would finally answer and Regis would ask,

"Is that your final answer?" the tension increased. A lot is at stake when you are dealing with a million-dollar question.

So, if Sunday didn't exist, would anyone know you were a follower of Jesus?

How do you feel dealing with that question? Nervous? Uncertain? Hesitant? Pressured? It is certainly a question worth taking seriously, but before you give your final answer, a caution needs to be given. With this question it is very possible to conclude that the end goal of our Christian lives is to be known as followers of Jesus. That is not the case. There is only one purpose for our being known.

That Jesus will be known.

Here, there, and everywhere.

By every man, woman, and child.

By every tribe, tongue, and nation.

That is the goal. That is the mission. That is the commission.

Go and make disciples of all nations, baptizing them in the name of the Father and of the Son and of the Holy Spirit, and teaching them to obey everything I have commanded you.

Matthew 28:19–20

And, oh, by the way, there is no Plan B. We are it. We are the ones.

Someone once said, "By ascending back up into heaven, Jesus took the risk of being forgotten by the world." I am not willing to let that happen. Are you?

Didn't think so.

So for his fame to grow, for him to be known, by everyone, we must be known.

So we are back to where we began. If Sunday didn't exist, would everyone know you are a follower of Jesus?

Would anyone?

That is the million-dollar question, and the question is not rhetorical.

⌐ Reflection/Discussion ⌐

1. If Sunday didn't exist, would anyone know you were a follower of Jesus? Why? Why not?

2. Be brave enough to ask someone close to you to answer the above question about you. Seek help in evaluating your life and identifying areas where Jesus may not be having his way with you. Invite continual accountability in order to follow Jesus well.

3. The mission and purpose of our lives is to make Jesus famous. Are you actively living toward that goal? If you are being passive with this responsibility, identify changes that need to take place in your life in order to live out this mission.

⌐ Prayer ⌐

Father, I pray that I will be known as your follower so I will have numerous opportunities to make sure you are known. There are so many in my workplace and neighborhood who need to know you. Through me or another one of your followers, make yourself known to them in an unmistakable way. I want to live for you in such a way that anyone, anywhere, would be able to identify me as your follower. Not for my fame, but for yours. In Jesus' name.

18

Dangerous

Many people, including my wife, are afraid of the ocean. The technical word for this type of fear is *thalassophobia*. I always dreamed of marrying a thalassophobic. I am sure there are numerous reasons why someone would be afraid of the ocean: the existence of sharks, the power of currents, the possibility of being eaten by a shark, the potential sting of a jellyfish, and the paralyzing thought of a dorsal fin suddenly appearing close by. By the way, galeophobia (the fear of sharks) hit pandemic levels in 1975, which happens to be the same year Jaws was released in theaters. Coincidence I am sure.

Interestingly, my wife's fear of the ocean has little to do with sharks. She would say it is the "unknown" of the ocean (though I think she is really just a galeophobic in disguise). People who study such things estimate that two-thirds of the earth's surface is covered by water, and that the oceans of the world hold approximately 326 quintillion gallons of water. Though extensive marine research goes on, and deep sea expeditions are common, the reality is that the ocean remains largely unknown.

When Jesus invites us to follow him, he is not inviting us to splash in a shallow puddle. He is inviting us to a journey into the deep unknown expanse of the ocean. The journey is not safe, or predictable, or measurable; following Jesus is dangerous, but it is only when you truly follow Jesus that *you* become dangerous.

Every time I hear, read, or write the word *dangerous*, I immediately think of the first church found in Acts and the few believers who sat together in a small upper room in Jerusalem. However, what began with a few believers quickly multiplied into thousands of believers. That is not a guess; it is a fact. In Acts 2, after Peter finished preaching, he gave an invitation, and as they stood and sang all four verses of "Just As I Am," about three thousand people responded by repenting of their sins and then were baptized in the name of Jesus Christ. Well, the song might not have been sung, but everything else happened.

And the Lord added to their number daily those who were being saved.

Acts 2:47

But many who heard the message believed; so the number of men who believed grew to about five thousand.

Acts 4:4

More and more men and women believed in the Lord and were added to their number.

Acts 5:14

I could go on and on quoting the Acts passages that directly or indirectly speak about the numerical growth of the church, but you can look those up on your own. My point is that the mid-first-century church is painted as being an influential, explosive, unstoppable, dangerous movement. Political and religious leaders of the day even accused the church of turning the world upside down in the name of Jesus (Acts 17:6). The believers were guilty as charged.

I would love to be accused of turning the world upside down in the name of Jesus. I hope the same for the church I serve. And for you.

However, for such an honorable accusation to be made about us, the world must be able to recognize that we live for Jesus. Our love for and commitment to Jesus must be obvious, apparent, evident, palpable, blatant, unmistakable, and every other synonym for these words.

Even if Sunday didn't exist.

⌐ Prayer ⌐

Father, as followers of you, and as your church, make us dangerous again. Teach us to live in such a way that the world around us cannot help but notice. May the power of the Holy Spirit be unleashed in us at such a noticeable level that we could be accused of turning the world upside down in the name of Jesus. Lord, we believe that what you did in the book of Acts can happen again, and we boldly ask, "Do it again, Lord, do it again." In Jesus' name.

Acknowledgments

Jenni, thank you for giving me an example of faith to follow.

Lakeside Christian Church, being your pastor is a joy and distinct privilege.

Craig Crynes, Jeff Breeze, and Kaycee Macy, thanks for the meaningful and helpful feedback early on in this process.

A huge thanks to Tim, Jeff, Brett, Carra, and the entire Bethany House/Baker team. *Real* would not have been possible without your talent and efforts. Working with all of you has been a real pleasure, no pun intended.

I feel like I am at the Oscars. The lights are dimming, the volume of the music is being raised, and yet I have so many people I would love to mention, so here goes. Dadio, I wouldn't be here without you. Kyle Idleman, thanks for always being in my corner. Mark Moore, thanks for giving me my first glimpses of who Jesus is and what he is like through your teaching. Deb Hafer, thanks for the hours you spent sharing loving truth with me. Matt Proctor, thanks for sharing your love and passion for preaching with me. Lakeside staff, I love working in the trenches of ministry with you every day. Hildegarde, my Tuesday afternoons will never be the same. I love you.

Jamie Snyder serves as lead pastor at Lakeside Christian Church. He and his wife, Alex, and their two sons live in Hebron, Kentucky. For more information, visit www.lakeside.org.